THREE FACES OF MOURNING:
MOURNING:
*Melancholia, Manic Defense,
and Moving On*

THREE FACES OF MOURNING

MOURNING

*Melancholia, Manic Defense,
and Moving On*

edited by

SALMAN AKHTAR, M.D.

JASON ARONSON

Lanham • Boulder • New York • Toronto • Plymouth, UK

A JASON ARONSON BOOK

ROWMAN & LITTLEFIELD PUBLISHERS, INC.

Published in the United States of America
by Rowman & Littlefield Publishers, Inc.
A wholly owned subsidiary of The Rowman & Littlefield Publishing Group, Inc.
4501 Forbes Boulevard, Suite 200, Lanham, Maryland 20706
www.rowmanlittlefield.com

Estover Road
Plymouth PL6 7PY
United Kingdom

British Library Cataloguing in Publication Information Available

**The hardback edition of this book was previously cataloged by the Library of Congress
as follows:**

Three faces of mourning : melancholia, manic defense, and moving on / edited by
Salman Akhtar.
       p. cm.
    Chiefly papers presented at the 32nd Annual Margaret S. Mahler Symposium
on Child Development, held Apr. 28, 2001 in Philadelphia, Pa.
    Includes bibliographical references and index.
    ISBN-13: 978-0-7657-0516-7 (pbk. : alk. paper)
    ISBN-10: 0-7657-0516-8 (pbk. : alk. paper)
    1.   Grief in children—Congresses. 2. Bereavement in children—
Congresses. 3. Children and death—Congresses. 4. Loss (Psychology) in
children—Congresses. 5. Grief—Congresses. 6. Bereavement—Psychological
aspects—Congresses. 7. Death—Psychological aspects—Congresses. 8. Loss
(Psychology)—Congresses. 9. Psychoanalysis—Congresses. 10. Freud,
Sigmund, 1856–1939—Congresses. I. Akhtar, Salman, 1946 July 31–
II. Margaret S. Mahler Symposium on Child Development (32nd : 2001 :
Philadelphia, Pa.)

BF723.G75 T47 2001
155.9'37'083—dc21   2001053736

Printed in the United States of America

♾™ The paper used in this publication meets the minimum requirements of American
National Standard for Information Sciences—Permanence of Paper for Printed Library
Materials, ANSI/NISO Z39.48-1992.

To the memory

of

Margaret S. Mahler

Teacher, friend, source of inspiration

Contents

Acknowledgments

The chapters in this book, with the exception of the Chapters 8 and 9, were originally presented as papers at the 32nd Annual Margaret S. Mahler Symposium on Child Development held on April 28, 2001, in Philadelphia. First and foremost, therefore, we wish to express our gratitude to the Margaret S. Mahler Psychiatric Research Foundation.

We are also grateful to Michael J. Vergare, M.D., Chairman of the Department of Psychiatry and Human Behavior, Jefferson Medical College, as well as to the Psychoanalytic Center of Philadelphia, for their shared sponsorship of the symposium. Many colleagues from the Center helped during the symposium, and we remain grateful to them.

Finally, we wish to acknowledge our sincere appreciation of Melissa Nevin for her efficient organization of and assistance during the symposium, and her outstanding skills in the preparation of this book's manuscript.

Contributors

Salman Akhtar, M.D.
Professor of Psychiatry, Jefferson Medical College; Training and Supervising Analyst, Psychoanalytic Center of Philadelphia

M. Hossein Etezady, M.D.
Clinical Director of Psychiatric Services, Paoli Memorial Hospital; Faculty, Psychoanalytic Center of Philadelphia

Theodore Fallon, Jr., M.D.
Clinical Associate Professor of Psychiatry, Hahnemann-Medical College of Pennsylvania; Advanced Candidate in Adult Psychoanalysis, Western New England Institute for Psychoanalysis; Candidate in Child Psychoanalysis, Psychoanalytic Center of Philadelphia

Corinne Masur, Psy.D.
Faculty, Psychoanalytic Center of Philadelphia; Private Practice of Adult and Child Psychotherapy and Psychoanalysis, Philadelphia

Helen Meyers, M.D.
Clinical Professor of Psychiatry, College of Physicians and Surgeons, Columbia University; Training and Supervising Analyst, Columbia University Center for Psychoanalytic Training and Research, New York

Henri Parens, M.D.

Professor of Psychiatry, Jefferson Medical College; Training and Supervising Analyst, Psychoanalytic Center of Philadelphia

Herbert Schlesinger, M.D.

Director, Department of Clinical Psychology, Columbia Presbyterian Center, New York; Supervising and Training Analyst, Columbia University Center for Psychoanalytic Training and Research, New York

Calvin F. Settlage, M.D.

Training and Supervising Analyst Emeritus in Adult and Child Analysis, San Francisco Psychoanalytic Institute; Clinical Professor of Psychiatry, University of California

William Singletary, M.D.

President, Margaret S. Mahler Psychiatric Research Foundation; Associate Faculty, Psychoanalytic Center of Philadelphia

WE ALL MOURN: C'EST LA CONDITION HUMANE

Henri Parens, M.D.

We all have mourned, do mourn, and will mourn: that is the human condition. But as the major chapters of this volume emphasize, mourning is not one thing. Much of it is not sad or bad; as I note below, this is so for those reactions that result from the psychic object losses that occur with normal developmental progression. Where mourning is sad, it documents that we love and have loved. Where it is bad, where it causes significant adaptive difficulty and symptoms, it is likely to follow losses such as of a valued part of the self as a leg or arm, or of one's fortune. In the case of libidinal object loss, among the most common conditions that make it "bad" are (1) where the loss occurs in early childhood and is not satisfactorily mourned and/or replaced, and (2) where the ambivalence attached to the lost object is high, such loss then will activate internalized object-attached rage that then especially will get directed toward both the object and the self. We know that object loss does many things to us. As quite a number of analysts have reported, the effects of loss may have long-lasting more or less troublesome effects (Fleming and Altschul 1963,

Furman 1974); it may leave positive or negative imprints on adaptation and character (Pollock 1961, Siggins 1966, Altschul 1968); and libidinal object loss may fuel and influence sublimation that yields remarkable creativity and unique productions (Wolfenstein 1974, Pollock 1989).

FREUD'S VIEWS ON MOURNING

Preoccupied as Freud was with death, according to Schur (1972) a lifelong preoccupation with him, it was only a matter of time before Freud would explore and try to understand the subject. In 1917 Freud conceptualized and described a theoretically cogent and clinically invaluable model of mourning (see also Bowlby 1961). It was easy for the practitioner and student of psychoanalysis to grasp Freud's model because it not only elucidated the work of mourning, but at the same time, it shed light on the process of "working through." To paraphrase Freud, the keystone process in mourning, and in working through, is to remember a psychic moment, to hypercathect it, analytically re-experience and metabolize it, and to decathect it. The model was and still is immediately comprehensible and clinically experience-near.

But in 1921, Freud reminded us that one of the key dynamic factors operative in mourning, the defense of identification, occurs at times other than in response to the loss of a libidinal object. Identification, he said, is "the earliest expression of an emotional tie with another person. . . . A little boy will exhibit a special interest in his father; he would like to grow like him and be like him, and take his place everywhere. . . . [H]e takes his father as his ideal" (p. 105). The father did not die. He simply was admired, loved. But Freud, as he was wont to do, did not leave it there. As he struggled with the limitations of the topographic model of the mind—that the mind can be thought of as constituted of a conscious, a preconscious, and an unconscious part—Freud (1923) came upon the Plato-derived[1] model of the mind that holds that it is constituted of three agencies, an id, an ego, and a superego, each with its unique functions. And in his continuing efforts to understand the evolving of the human child's mind, in 1923 he addressed the organization, development, and functions of the ego (Chapter 3) and the superego (Chapter 5). He proposed that as the child progressed from one developmental phase to the next, he gains in development but he loses libidinal elements of the past. While the gain of that phasic progression brings with it the advance beyond the earlier achieved development, at the same time this advance brings with it the loss or abandonment of the prior phase's experiences and of the specific object-cathexes contained in these earlier phase experiences. Thinking in psychosexual terms, one could for clarification purposes oversimplify this to mean that the "oral phase mother" is (relatively) lost to the child when the child moves into the anal phase. And Freud wondered if in this process, "identification is the sole condition under which the id can give up its objects" (p. 29). This led Freud to propose, in conceptualizing the development of the ego, that "the character of the ego is a precipitate of abandoned object cathexes and that it contains the history of those object-choices" (p. 29). In this, Freud held that normal development brings the child face-to-face with repeated libidinal-object losses that activate some elements of mourning. Helen Meyers makes this point in telling us that the loss of "the mother of symbiosis" during the Rapprochement subphase induces a "pseudo-mourning reaction Mahler identified as *lowkeyedness*" (Chapter 2). Thus, object loss and the work of mourning it brings with it reaches well beyond the experience of actual libidinal-object loss.

---

[1]Plato in his Republic conceptualized the city as being essentially constituted of 3 classes of citizens: (1) the bon vivants, sinners, and thieves; (2) the police and courts; and (3) the wise teachers and governors. I am indebted for this information to Erik F. Parens and Joshua S. Parens.

That development brings with it loss has now been well established. A sweeping overview of a life span reveals that evidence of loss or the threat of loss starts from near the beginning of life. In the process of attachment (Bowlby 1969), the structuring of the libidinal object (Spitz 1965) is confirmed in the 6- to 12-month-old's acute reaction to the threat of loss, that is in separation anxiety. And this crucial development carries with it the full-blown potential for an "anaclitic depression" (Spitz 1946) if the child actually loses the object as through death or, as Spitz saw it through maternal incarceration for criminal behavior, or psychologically loses the object as may occur in maternal postpartum depression. M. Klein's (1939) temporally coincident "depressive position" gains support in these observable behavioral phenomena.

In 1926 Freud, framing it in the psychosexual model, proposed his series of developmentally timed sequential threats of loss: fear of object loss (oral phase), fear of loss of the object's love (anal phase), fear of loss of a highly narcissistically invested part of the self (phallic phase), and the fear of loss of love of the superego (latency phase). Continuing this loss series, from contributors who followed Freud we can add the loss of the parents of childhood (an arduous task of adolescence), the loss of home on going into young adulthood, to the loss of one's own children when they leave home to go into the world (to which many a mother reacts with actual depression), to menopause, to retirement from work, and to loss of health and loss of mate in the late years. These emotional losses that are part of our normal life course center around the loss of love-objects or the loss of a component of self.

But psychological loss is well known to be experienced in other spheres as well. We could say that the loss of any emotionally invested animate (human, pet animal) or inanimate (fortune, jewelry, etc.) or part object (one's arm, leg), or place (home, country) or position (job, in family [the first born when another sibling comes into the family, parent of grown children], in the community) brings with it the experience of psychological loss. Each engenders mourning. We can add to Zetzel's (1965) telling us that we all must be able to bear the depression loss brings; we all must also be able to bear the mourning emotional loss requires. But do we all agree that emotional loss requires that we mourn?

THE VIEWS OF MEYERS, SETTLAGE, AND SCHLESINGER

Helen Meyers wonders if it does. Meyers opened the symposium with two key questions. Meyers narrows her focus sharply and first asks what does the loss of her mother do to a woman? Her answer, very worthy of thought, begins an inquiry that will go on well beyond what she says about it. With this generative question she opens up unexplored territory. What about men? What does it mean for a man to lose his mother? Is it different? What about when the woman loses her father? And men for that matter too? And perhaps most forbidding, what about the woman, the mother who loses her child? And the father who loses his child? Bedrich Smetana wrote his most heart rending piano trio (in G minor, opus 15) following the loss of one of his young children. Meyers brings many questions to mind; I will only ask some of these questions. Helen Meyers does me one better; she addresses her question.

Meyers does more. She questions the idea I laid out in the preceding paragraphs. She asks "Is mourning necessary?" We know that many people avoid mourning. But I have not heard an analyst ask this question. This too deserves our attention. The author–questioner is brave. Just as I am writing these introductory pages I heard a program on Public Radio International entitled "Sound and Spirit" in which Host Helen Kushner (2001) reports on mourning practices throughout the world. The range of underlying beliefs and philosophies, mores and rituals is startlingly wide. It is not just analysts who will pay attention on hearing Helen Meyers' question.

In his chapter, Calvin F. Settlage first focuses on libidinal loss of relationship with mother as a normal and a pathogenic experience in early childhood, and second on the relationship of pathologically experienced childhood loss to the adult capacity to mourn the actual loss of a loved one. What is the meaning of loss when, as Settlage points out, that evolution had embedded love into human nature and development? Settlage does not simply say this; he draws on cumulative findings of many developmentalists from within and outside of psychoanalysis. He draws well the dimensions of object loss when he tells us that the critical psychobiologically driven libidinal attachment, "the symbiotic, affective relationship," is what is lost. This loss is experienced most painfully, and he tells us it generates much hostile destructiveness in the child. The link between object loss and hostile destructiveness is well known to us since Freud first explained it in *Mourning and Melancholia* (1917). Settlage emphasizes that the repression of aggression is a key factor in pathogenic formations that follow on object loss, and that this cannot only produce symptoms but also interfere with normal development. He calls our attention to this and documents it with vignettes from clinical work that followed on his moving from California to Arkansas.

While preparing to leave the city where for years Settlage was treating patients, several of them resisted discontinuing talking with him and elected to continue their clinical work with him long distance, both by telephone and occasionally by seeing him when he returned for visits to said city. In his chapter, Settlage reports on three patients who elected to work with him in this way. He reports briefly on his finding that his patients had great difficulty expressing the hostility they experienced at his having left them. His helping them find ways to recognize and express these feelings toward him led them to achieve relief from symptoms. From this and no doubt many years of clinical and observational experience, Settlage proposes that the status of aggression as pathogen needs to be elevated in psychoanalysis to the pathogenic status we have given to sexuality. My clinical and observational experience strongly supports this position.

Herbert Schlesinger's chapter is vintage Schlesinger. He is

clear, like Anna Freud is deceptively simple and sensitive, all the while being richly informing, educational, and philosophic. For example, Schlesinger tells us that significant loss is never fully expunged while mourning is episodic. He addresses two major points in one breath: (1) Do we ever fully mourn the loss of a primary love-object? Does the assumption that "the earliest cathexes are indelible," which Freud (1939) asserted at the end of his life, hold? Schlesinger takes a position on this point. And, (2) he questions what we expect of patients who are mourning: Does the work of mourning proceed on a continuous course? How far can mourning itself go?

Schlesinger looks at our work with patients who are mourning and addresses some technical implications of it. For instance, should we interpret the work of mourning? But perhaps more far-reaching, Schlesinger asks us to be attentive to our own defensiveness against mourning in our patients. He highlights a major challenge to the analyst when working with a patient who is mourning. Following on years of supervision and consultation Schlesinger tells us that some clinicians have difficulty tolerating seeing their patients in pain. It is common to wish to spare our loved ones, including our patients and ourselves, pain of any kind, and we may feel impelled to alleviate *our* distress by intervening to ameliorate *their* suffering. We must allow a patient to feel the pain of loss in order to permit the patient to mourn. It is a critical point Schlesinger makes. It may not have gotten the attention we should pay to it. And it is an issue that requires caution in what we recommend among ourselves and especially to our younger colleagues. We must allow and therewith help the patient come to tolerate naturally painful events to be experienced as painful. But we cannot induce pain that does not follow from the actual course that life fate has handed our patients. We can no more allow our countertransference to disallow the normal experience of pain of loss or other trauma, than we can allow our countertransference to cause our patients pain. I shall return to this point shortly.

Schlesinger talks about three contexts in which the analyst can expect to encounter mourning: (1) when the patient suffers the loss of a significant other; (2) when the patient loses a part of the self; and (3) when the patient has resolved some issue of analytic importance sufficiently that the ensuing change carries with it an intimation that the analysis will some day end. Schlesinger discusses these in detail.

Schlesinger's observation on how the intolerance for pain we feel may lead us to interfere with our patients' working through the experience object loss reaches wide around us. In my work I too have found this problem not only among those we supervise and where we do consultations, but I have also found it among adults vis-à-vis children, especially their own. In Chapter 8, I address just this question. But I address it from the point of view of its occurrence in children and of its implications for mental health prevention. I try to do so by (1) drawing awareness to the pathogenic potential brought about by such pain intolerance in parents and other child caregivers, and (2) by pointing to the pathogenic potential that lies in our not recognizing that disallowing the child to feel the pain of loss interferes with the child's ability to mourn.

CONCLUSION

As is the custom of the symposium, each presentation is formally discussed. Corinne Masur discussed Helen Meyers' presentation. She especially addressed Meyers' questioning the need to mourn, expanding and further bringing to view the issue for our own considerations of it. Discussing Settlage's presentation, Salman Akhtar, well known for his erudition, writings, and pedagogical skills, furthered Settlage's exposition by adding to it enriching details and ideas put forth by other analytic thinkers as well as his own. William Singletary took up Schlesinger's presentation finding support from his own clinical work and readings for the presenter's thesis and duly acknowledging Schlesinger's clinical–pedagogical thoughts and recommendations to us. We believe that the experience the symposium participants and attendees reported comes through in these pages; the reader stands to be further informed and enriched by their perusal.

REFERENCES

Altschul, S. (1968). Denial and ego arrest. *Journal of the American Psychoanalytic Association* 16:301–318.

Bowlby, J. (1961). Process of mourning. *International Journal of Psycho-Analysis* 42:317–340.

———. (1969). *Attachment*. New York: Basic Books.

Fleming, J. and Altschul, S. (1963). Activation of mourning and growth by psycho-analysis. *International Journal of Psycho-Analysis* 44:419–431.

Freud, S. (1917). Mourning and melancholia. *Standard Edition* 14:237–258.

———. (1921). Group psychology and the analysis of the ego. *Standard Edition* 18:67–143.

———. (1923). The ego and the id. *Standard Edition* 19:3–66.

———. (1926). Inhibition, symptoms and anxiety. *Standard Edition* 20:77–174.

———. (1939). An outline of psychoanalysis. *Standard Edition* 23:141–207.

Furman, E. (1974). *A Child's Parent Dies*. New Haven, CT: Yale University Press.

Klein, M. (1939). *The Psychoanalysis of Children*. New York: Grove Press, 1960.

Kushner, H., Host (2001). *"Sound and Spirit—Mourning across cultures."* Public Radio International, May 27, 2001.

Pollock, G. H. (1961). Mourning and adaptation. *International Journal of Psycho-Analysis* 42:341–361.

———. (1989). *The Mourning-Liberation Process*, Vols. 1 & 2. Madison, CT: International Universities Press.

Schur, M. (1972). *Freud: Living and Dying*. New York: International Universities Press.

Siggins, L. D. (1966). Mourning: a critical review of the literature. *International Journal of Psycho-Analysis* 47:14–23.

Spitz, R. (1946). Anaclitic depression: An inquiry into the genesis of psychiatric conditions in early childhood. *The Psychoanalytic Study of the Child* 2:313–342.

———. (1965). *The First Year of Life*. New York: International Universities Press.

Wolfenstein, M. (1974). The past recaptured in the work of Rene Magritte. Presented at the 5th Annual Margaret S. Mahler Symposium, Philadelphia, PA, May 1974.

Zetzel, E. R. (1965). Depression and the incapacity to bear it. In *Drives, Affects, Behavior, 2,* ed. M. Schur, pp. 243–274. New York: International Universities Press.

2

DOES MOURNING BECOME ELECTRA? OEDIPAL AND SEPARATION-INDIVIDUATION ISSUES IN A WOMAN'S LOSS OF HER MOTHER

Helen Meyers, M.D.

A great deal has been written about mourning in the psychoanalytic literature: "healthy" mourning (Freud 1917), pathologic mourning (Volkan 1981), mourning in children on loss of a parent (Nagera 1970), and the impact of early object loss on later personality development and particularly on the occurrence of pathologic mourning later in life. Indeed, the similarity between adult pathologic mourning and "normal" childhood mourning (Wolfenstein 1966, 1969) has been noted. The importance of going through the complete mourning process has been stressed in pointing out the dangers of bypassing mourning by denial, "absence of mourning," and displaced mourning, which is likely to lead to constriction of functioning, inability to form new in-depth attachments, prolonged depression, or other symptom formation.

In general, the normal mourning process, as differentiated from pathologic mourning or melancholia, has been conceptualized along two major lines: 1) As championed by Freud (1917), who sees the process as identification with, or internalization of the lost object into the ego, which is raged against by the superego; the internalized object is then slowly decathected bit by bit until it is totally divested of libidinal investment and energy is freed for new external object attachments. Thus, first we would have anger, anger directed at the self, that is depression, then painful detachment from the internalized object, and finally acceptance of the loss and availability for new attachments. 2) As proposed by Bowlby (1960, 1963, 1969), the process first involves non-acceptance of the loss with attempts at retrieving the lost object by angry demands and crying; secondly, awareness of the loss, causing disorganization of the internal structure; and finally, reorganization with the acceptance of the loss. Thus, in both conceptualizations the manifestations of mourning involve three phases: angry protest, externally or internally directed; disorganization or internal detachment; and finally, reorganization or letting go. However, the mechanisms are conceptualized differently with Freud stressing identification and decathexis and Bowlby stressing yearning and attempts at regaining the object.

I have very little to add to this rich literature and understanding, so I would like to use this opportunity to speculate on an idea I have, based on my clinical experience and elaborated by my own theory, and raise a perhaps provocative question. What I want to speculate about is an intriguing issue not, to my knowledge, much dealt with in the literature concerning mourning in an adult woman upon the loss of her mother. How do women deal with the loss of mother? Obviously, different women will deal differently with the loss of mother depending on their individual dynamics and relationship with mother, and I will try to give some examples of this. However, do they have something in common? Is there anything universal, specific, special, or different about the loss of mother for a woman in adulthood (not in childhood) and without previous object loss in childhood, different from the loss of father, and different from a man's reaction to the loss of mother? If so, how can we think about it? Can we relate it to the separation-individuation process and early identifications and disidentifications? Finally I will question the necessity of classical "mourning" for a "healthy" resolution in dealing with object loss as universally accepted in the analytic literature. Thus, the title of my contribution is "Does Mourning Become Electra?" Of course, my question on the necessity of going through the stages of mourning after object loss concerns not only women, but men as well.

ADULT WOMEN MOURNING THEIR MOTHERS' DEATH

Based on my clinical experience, I am suggesting that, in general, women deal with the death of their father as the loss of an "Other"—a beloved other if they had a good relationship with father, a not loved other if they had an ambivalent relationship— but always an other, while they deal with the death of mother as a loss of part of themselves. Here is how I think about it. During the separation-individuation process (Mahler et al. 1975), girls and boys internalize aspects of mother, and later of father as well. These internalizations remain as object representations or add to the self-representations via identification. Later, of course, some of these internalized images enter into superego formation. Girls particularly identify with mother in the formation of gender identity while separating from the real mother as external object. Boys, however, have to disidentify with mother (Greenson 1968) and identify with father to attain their male gender identity. At the same time, rapprochement involves the threat of loss of the mother of separation, or the loss of the love of the mother of separation, which also is defended against by identification, as well as mitigated against by yearning for, and actively, vociferously going after the real mother; depression, shadowing, and crying are observed manifestations of this. Thus, this period can be thought of as first "pseudo" mourning, potential mourning, or prototype of mourning, involving elements described by both Freud and Bowlby as essential in mourning; that is, identification with the lost object (Freud) and yearning and aggressively trying to retrieve the lost object (Bowlby). Girls, however, according to my theoretical assumption, shared by others, remain less separated from the actual mother. This recalls Freud's observation and formulation about superego formation. There, as you know, he suggests that the male superego, that is the internalization of the parental images at the end of the oedipal period motivated by castration anxiety, is much stronger, complete, and abstract than the girl's superego motivated by separation anxiety alone. This, according to Freud, was not as strong a motivator as castration anxiety, particularly since he felt that daughters never fully separated from mothers anyway, and thus the threat of separation, separation anxiety, was not as powerful. Of course, while I obviously disagree with Freud's conclusion about the incompleteness or weakness of the female superego, which I feel is fully as strong and functioning as a man's, though it has a different content of ideas and ideals, his observation of the incomplete separation of mother and daughter seems related to my previous formulation. Thus, it would appear that mother continues to serve a kind of self-object function, continuing to empathically mirror the girl's self-assertion and needs and lending herself as an object of identification.

Furthermore, the ambitendency of the rapprochement phase develops into ambivalence, particularly in the girl in the oedipal phase in competition with mother. Thus, in addition to the girl's identification with the maternal introject for individuation and identity formation and the incomplete separation from mother, as described above, the competitive oedipal ambivalence towards mother further gives impetus to the oedipal and post-oedipal girl's need to hold on to the external mother and not to separate too much for fear of punishment by the loss of mother.

The way I look at it, in adolescence there is a second period of a kind of "pseudo" mourning as described earlier for the period of separation individuation. There is a push towards internal object removal as well as separation from the external mother in adolescence with the threat of loss, with periods of depression and internal disorganization, as well as yearning for attachment as described in Bowlby's mourning process. At the same time, however, there is also again a greater push for the girl to identify with mother, in formation of her identity, particularly her sexual and gender identity and role; thus, leading to internal psychic reorganization of the ego, ego ideal and superego, and also fitting Freud's description of part of the mourning process that involves identification. Again, the separation of daughter from mother is not so complete, with the mother continuing to serve a self-object function throughout her lifetime. Thus, I am suggesting that the girl's larger self representation includes both internalized aspects of the maternal object, as well as aspects of the still external mother. After all, as we know, Erikson's (1956) ego or self identity includes self concepts over time, the self seen in relation to others, and the way others see our self.

In adulthood then, with the actual loss of the older parent, the normal mourning, involving yearning, seeking to retrieve the object, partial denial, sadness and grief, and identification, that is protest, grieving, disorganization and reorganization or "manic defense, melancholia, and moving on" is really, in a way, a third time around based on the two previous periods of pseudo mourning or prototypes in normal development; this is without the occurrence of actual object loss in childhood which, according to many authors, often impinges pathologically on personality development in general, and may lead to pathologic mourning in adult object loss.

Based on this conceptualization of developmental repetition in girls of the defensive identification with mother in the two previous stages, as well as the girl's less complete separation from the external mother who continues to serve more of a self-object function, I am proposing, as stated in the beginning of this paper, that mourning differs for the woman in reaction to the loss of mother versus the loss of father. She deals with the death of father as to the loss of an "Other," beloved or otherwise, while she deals with the death of mother as a loss of part of her Self. This Self, as I have suggested, includes the internalized mother as well as, in a larger sense, the self-object function part of the real external mother still attached to the self-image. This is so, regardless of whether the overt relationship with mother was loving or conflictual, positive or negative, and even if the girl had been overtly closer to father in a more loving and adoring relationship. With the death of such a father there may be yearning, crying, grief, temporary unwillingness to let him go, imagining seeing him on street corners, or having dreams where he is alive, ending with an acceptance of the reality of his death, yet continuing to think about him in various circumstances. In other words, this has all the elements of mourning for a *separate* beloved person.

When the mother dies, however, I believe there is a greater internal change involving a sense of having lost part of oneself, a sense of having lost the early caretaking mother who has continued as a needed self object throughout life. There may or may not also be the expected aspects of mourning as described previously such as crying, grief, protest, disorganization, and so on. Of course, there are also apt to be specific major differences in the manifestations of mourning in different women depending on their dynamics, psychopathology, and relationship with mother. But I am suggesting that they have in common an internal change, the sense of loss of part of the self that was partially a "mother within" or an open-ended connection with the external mother in her continued need-fulfilling function as described above. This may be dealt with by filling in the loss in the greater self by identification, a kind of "becoming" mother. This may manifest itself in a variety of ways from temporary assumption of activities that mother used to be involved in, to more permanent attitudinal changes and sense of self.

THREE CLINICAL EXAMPLES

Case 1

A reasonably well-adjusted, mildly neurotic, reasonably successful, happily married woman with children, with reasonable separateness from the parents, and with no background of major trauma or losses in her early childhood or later development, lost her mother at age 50. Throughout her life she had been identified with both parents in ideals and ambitions, as well as having the usual oedipal conflicts. Both parents were professionals, and the daughter followed into that professional life successfully as well. Although she had a good, though separate, relationship with both parents, she was closer to her father who adored her while mother, at times also admiring of the daughter, seemed to favor the son. Our patient identified with the father's intellectualism, values, and ambitions, but also identified with mother's charm and grace and social interactions with others. When the father died, some years before her mother, the patient reacted with a short period of pain, grief, and yearning, wishing he had not died, although there was never any question of non-acceptance of the reality. This experience was brief and never interfered with her functioning. During this early period, she occasionally dreamt of father being alive and having conversations with him in which he was loving and supportive and gave good advice. When she returned from exciting travels, she thought of telling him the details of the experience, which she had always done while he was alive. She missed these conversations, as she missed many other pleasurable interactions with him. On one occasion when she felt unappreciated by her husband, the thought burst into her head that "only father really loved me."

When mother died, there also was a brief period of pain and grief, as well as some specific feelings of guilt of not having been extra attentive during the last month of mother's illness when she was living in the daughter's home. When the daughter found the mother, who had died during the night, there was momentary denial, the daughter thinking the mother was asleep or in a coma and did not recognize the death until the husband had to point it out to her. This was thus a gross denial of the reality for a few minutes but did not continue as such, although it took her several years to put an inscription on the gravestone, which I think represented an attempt at unconscious denial of the reality of the death. Of course, it could also have represented some ambivalence since she knew how much these formalities meant to her mother, more than to father.

The interesting thing, however, was that she, a little bit, "became" mother without at first recognizing this identification. She started to do needlepoint and knitting, activities she had never taken up before but which her mother had enjoyed; the mother had made many garments and pillows for her daughter. Furthermore, although our patient was always a good hostess, she unwittingly enlarged her parties with musical offerings, an activity her mother was well known for, having been a chanteuse herself who performed at her famous social gatherings. This could, of course, be seen as a "manic defense," but I believe the identification was the more important mechanism.

She also became mildly irritable, which had not been evident before but which had been part of the mother's makeup. Again this could be looked at as the appearance of anger or protest, but again I find identification a better explanation. She also began to walk somewhat stooped as her mother had, and, although slim all her life, she began to put on weight as her mother had always been quite plump. This could be put down to the woman growing older and having physical changes in relation to hormonal changes in menopause, but again I do not find that as a sufficient explanation.

As with her father, she did recall mother with a sense of missing her at certain occasions, but these had to do with the preoedipal caretaking mother: when indisposed she had a sense of longing for the touch of her mother's soft skin and specially prepared food that mother prepared for her when she was ill in her early childhood. There was no depression or change in mood, but there was a conscious sense that remained of being now without mother, of being motherless in this world. Of course, I believe that with the death of either parent there is a sense of difference in the world; not like the feelings on the death of a spouse or dearly beloved friend which may be equally or more painful, but a sense of now being the responsible older generation, no longer the child looking for the parents' generation to take care of things, a kind of partial emptiness, a sense of finiteness of life, as well as a feeling of maturity and being the CEO in charge.

For our patient, this experience did not really take hold until the death of her mother, although, as I said above, she had greatly missed her father when he died. So, while there was no impairment of functioning or change in general mood or functioning, and the period of painful affect was quite brief with the loss of mother, I believe there was a sense of a permanent internal change, a sense of loss of a small part of her Self or the larger self that had included the mother—the space being filled in with internalization or identification with mother.

Case 2

This patient presented a very different story. She had an enormously attached, dependent, and ambivalent relationship with mother. The father was more shadowy and in the background, adoring of mother and always telling the daughter to listen to and make up with mother. An accomplished sculptress, the mother was demanding, clever, charming, and totally self-absorbed. She obviously preferred the two boys, as she called them "extraordinary Eddie" and "marvelous Max," while the patient was referred to as "good Suzie." While the patient adored these younger brothers and took great care of them in her youth, in her later adulthood she grew to resent and hate them, almost going into a panic whenever they visited New York and thus threatened her current special union with her mother, as she was devoting her life to trying to become mother's favorite and "only" child, an attempt in which she failed, of course.

In high school, the patient developed a talent in painting that she pursued with great joy in art school, but stopped when she started dating men in her 20s. Reconstructing this, it appeared that in her oedipal competition and guilty inhibition of assertion, she unconsciously allowed herself only to get a little pleasure from either artistic self-expression *or* sexual expression, and one had to be given up for the other. However, the pleasure attained in either had to be limited and not lead to full gratification in that she could only enjoy sex with men who either treated her badly or were unavailable, and in terms of her art, she would not permit herself to experiment freely with or finish or show her paintings. She, thus, gave up much of her oedipal competition and became submissive—rather textbook oedipal dynamics.

Once married, she became an extra "good" wife, mother, and friend, always bringing two kinds of cakes to every party, feeding everybody at numerous parties, and in general, taking care of everybody, as well as continuing to be a good daughter. Secretly, but consciously, she was furious at everybody as nobody was taking care of her, but she felt very guilty about this anger, tried to deny it, and then would double her efforts at "goodness." Sexually, she could not permit herself any pleasure or gratification with her husband except when they went to some shabby hotel on occasional weekends where she felt somewhat mischievous and a bit like a prostitute.

In relation to her mother, her conflict between overt submissiveness and suppressed anger was doubly strong. She called her mother twice every day, had her for dinner every Sunday, took her on every trip abroad, and worked for her mother in her store where mother sold some of her sculptures, thinking that she adored mother, who was quite marvelous. There she was a good saleswoman for her mother and spent her time admiring her mother, who spent her time showing off to her daughter the wonderful work she did. However, the patient was becoming more aware of her secret fury at her mother, who did not let her develop a sense of worth and self, and did not help her to individuate and become independent; but the patient would not dare to express this openly for fear of mother's anger and the fear that her adored and needed mother would desert her.

Secretly, she yearned for sexual pleasure and to again pursue her own creative work as a painter, which she consciously pretended she was not able to pursue with the excuse of lack of time in the service of her mother and her children. These discontents, indeed, were the reasons she came into treatment at the age of 40. During treatment, she began to tentatively return to painting but only in the classroom under the tutelage of an admired woman instructor, and she began to have some tentative sexual pleasure. She also attempted to speak up to mother about not continuing to work in the store and about her need to develop her own existence. But she became panicky and depressed when she spoke to her mother. Her mother's reaction was anger and hurt, accusing the patient of not loving her. The patient tried to stick to her guns and refused to call her mother to apologize as her father had always made her do. However, she could not handle this. She cried, became somewhat confused, could not pursue her usual activities, and got into angry fights with her husband and children, fearing that her mother would never speak to her again and she would lose her mother's love forever.

After two weeks she called her mother, invited her to dinner and the theatre, and was enormously relieved when mother accepted. She then re-assumed her "friendly, cheerful" false self, guiltily returned to being a dutiful daughter and went back to work. When mother died, the therapist expected a strong reaction to this major loss with much guilt and depression as well as a sense of disorganization. However, on the contrary, the patient reacted with relief and a sense of freedom. She took over the mother's store, selling the remainder of mother's sculptures as well as some of her own paintings. After a while she lost interest in the store and devoted herself full time to her adored painting, having converted the upper floor in her house into a studio where she was now able to paint on her own without the help of an instructor, and successfully entered her paintings in competitive shows. She also experienced greater sexual freedom and began to be orgastic in regular intercourse with her husband. There was no regression from this position as she went on, but there was a permanent sense of change in her internal self concept from the "daughter" position to "complete" woman, the "mother of the family" who no longer had a mother of her own. She, thus, did not go through the normal mourning process, nor were there any expected negative sequellae.

This appears to be certainly not a pathologic solution but a happy ending, but it did involve a sense of inner shift, a sense of never being the same again. Now, if we were psychologically unsophisticated we might have said: "Of course, she was relieved at the disappearance of this noxious influence of mother." As analysts, however, we would wonder what happened to the enormous guilt we would have expected, at the fantasy of "killing off" her oedipal competitive and preoedipal domineering mother, as well as enormous helplessness at losing the needed external mother. Thus, we would have expected perhaps rage, depression, and disorganization.

However, the way I look at it, what I think happened is that the patient internalized the lost mother, identified with her, and "became" the competent mother. She became the owner of the store instead of the denigrated salesgirl, and now, as the mother, was permitted to express her artistic ability as mother had and to be a sexually grown woman. Thus, I am suggesting that she, in this way, completed and solidified her own self-identity, which now included identification with the internal and external mother, and she no longer needed the self-object function of the mother.

There are, of course, other versions of dealing differently with this sense of loss of part of the self. One patient, for instance, had a close loving relationship with mother throughout adulthood without any conscious ambivalence, where any anger or competition was totally repressed. She did not fill in for the lost internal and external mother with new identification and "becoming" mother (she was already greatly identified with mother), but by proceeding with a more usually accepted picture of mourning for the external object. There was prolonged grieving, though without cessation of functioning. She continued to visit the grave frequently, perhaps weekly, silently talking to mother, and getting a sense of comfort by the continued "presence" of the mother, though there was no impairment in reality testing and the awareness that mother, indeed, was dead. There was a feeling that mother was gone but not forgotten and that it would have pleased mother to know she was not forgotten. This then would be a more external mourning rather than an internalization. This woman, however, also after this prolonged mourning, continued to have a sense of being different, "motherless," as I described in the other cases.

Case 3

To counterpoint the above "healthy" resolutions of the loss of mother, let me quickly present another situation with a more pathologic outcome: The patient was an only daughter whose father deserted her mother in the patient's early years. This, of course, constituted a kind of early object loss that, it has been suggested, often leads to a pathologic mourning process later in life. The mother, feeling helpless and desperate, married another man who could take care of her and who she expected to provide financial and emotional support, which he apparently did. The stepfather, however, started to molest the child, continuing through her early teens, paying her with gifts and money.

The girl accepted this painful situation silently without telling mother, who supposedly never knew of the situation and certainly never did anything to stop it. The patient left home to go to college, where she was a good student and entered the academic profession. She was married in her early 20s, somewhat unhappily, and proceeded with a fairly successful academic career. When the mother died, somewhat prematurely, the patient left her husband and academia and became a high-class prostitute.

On the surface this looked simply like a repetition of her early experience with the stepfather, but on closer examination in analysis, it became clear that there were two elements related to mother. One was her intense suppressed fury at her mother, as she felt mother must have known about what was going on sexually with the stepfather and had not protected her. This prostitution activity was revenge against the phony middle-class morality and ambition of her mother, who had admired her academic bent. The other element was that she felt mother, herself, had been a prostitute in that she sold herself and her daughter to this man (stepfather) for money and security. She, thus, on the death of her mother identified with her mother as a prostitute saying overtly "I am now the same as her." Thus, in her pathologic angry way this patient also held on to mother and dealt with the loss by internalizing the lost object and identified with her.

A PROVOCATIVE QUESTION?

It appears universally accepted in psychoanalytic writings that it is essential to go through the whole normal mourning process after the loss of a parent to avoid a traumatic impact impinging on further development or the existing personality structure. In contrast, a pathologic reaction could involve denial of mourning; displaced mourning onto other people, animals, or possessions; rage; prolonged grief or depression or melancholia, manic defense, particularly constriction of avoidance of new intimate object relations; acting out in perversion or promiscuity; or other symptom formation. The literature on "normal" mourning is rich and most convincing, and it ranges from the classical to the modern, that is from Freud, through Bowlby, to Furman (1974).

I would, however, like to question this inevitability. Of course, I believe that many people do go through all or some of the steps of mourning to resolve their loss, but many others, I believe, do not and come out none the worse for wear. I have given some examples of both in this paper. Here is my thinking about this: Freud described the normal process of mourning as internalization of the ambivalently held lost object into the ego in order to keep the external object now internally, as well as to express the anger at the object now as superego rage against the object now within the ego. This is followed by slow decathexis of the object with the libido withdrawn from it, thus freeing the energy to be invested in another object. This would be a healthy resolution.

Now I disagree with the need to decathect the internalized object. This, of course, was part of Freud's old outmoded theory of the U2 conceptualization of there being only a defined limited quantity of libido, which is invested either in the object or the self. A theory, I presume, none of us subscribe to any more since we do not believe there is a limited amount of love to go around. It is obviously quite possible to invest a new object with love and feeling while maintaining the attachment to the internal object as well. In fact, one of the basis of my concepts presented in this paper is that internalization of the object that remains invested, identification with mother for the woman, that is "becoming mother," and, thus, filling in the lost part of the self, makes for the special resolution of the trauma of the loss of mother for the adult woman and obviates, not bypasses, the mourning that involves rage and depression and functional interference. Indeed, I cannot understand the suggestion that the internal object has to be decathected as if one should not maintain loving attachment and memories of mother and the relationship in order to move on. Clearly, of course, if the woman were preoccupied with the lost relationship, unable to think of anything else or re-attach, or function normally, that would constitute one form of pathologic mourning.

As for Bowlby's description of the three phases of mourning—protest, disorganization, and reorganization—this certainly was evidenced in the children he observed in World War II and has been observed in others, children and adults alike. But in my experience it has not been observed in all adults with object loss, who did not go through rage or disorganization, nor experience pathologic substitutes such as denial, manic defense, and others as described previously. I believe that this is true in two of the cases I described in this paper: both the woman who took up needlepoint and the woman who became an artist. In both cases I believe that there was a sense of loss of part of the self that was resolved and filled in by internalization and unconscious identification of the self with mother, constituting a continued attachment to this internalized image, as well as producing an internal change in the self leading to a strengthened and now more complete self-concept. There was continued good functioning or even improved functioning as in Case 2, while, at the same time, there *was* a continued awareness of the permanent absence of the mother, a sense of motherlessness, memories of the interactions with mother, and continued attachment to these memories.

Another set of authors who have written a great deal on parental death and mourning, the Furman (1974), go a step further on the necessity of going through the mourning process after

parental loss, particularly in childhood. They even propose that
children should be taught the meaning of death and loss and the
attendant mourning processes including showing them dead animals and helping them express their anger, sorrow, and bewilderment. I have questions about this in that I think it may force
children into an emotional experience that, while meant to release
what is suppressed and repressed to avoid traumatic damage, may
not have been there in the first place and *create* a traumatic effect
that would otherwise not have been there. This, of course, addresses
the old question related to different theories of technique: whether
bringing out in the patient, in the transference, certain feelings like
rage, helplessness, guilt, or overwhelming sexual desires is always
the uncovering or release of these hidden suppressed or unconscious feelings—a desirable objective—or whether it is an introduction of these feelings into the analytic situation, by suggestion,
projection, or seduction by the analyst. It is well known for
instance that Kohut (1972) feels that the rage reaction in narcissistic patients is often created by the non-empathic intervention
by the analyst, while object relations theorists suggest that it is an
essential aspect of technique to release the already present, repressed, damaging rage by the appropriate interpretation.

The patients I refer to then never went through the full
processes as described by Bowlby, Freud, and Furman, and yet two
of them achieved a good continued functioning, though with
some internal changes. Does this not suggest that our notions
regarding mourning need some reconsideration and revision?

REFERENCES

Bowlby, J. (1960). Grief and mourning in infancy and early childhood. *The Psychoanalytic
Study of the Child*, 15:9–52.

———. (1963). Pathological mourning and childhood mourning. *Journal of the American
Psychoanalytic Association* 11:500–541.

———. (1969). *Attachment and Loss. Vol. 1: Attachment*. New York: Basic Books.

Erikson, E.H. (1956). The problem of ego identity. *Journal of the American Psychoanalytic Association* 4:56–121.

Freud, S. (1917). Mourning and melancholia. *Standard Edition* 14:237–258.

Furman, E. (1974). *A Child's Parent Dies.* New Haven, CT: Yale University Press.

Greenson, R. (1968). Dis-identitfying from mother: its special importance for the boy. *International Journal of Psycho-Analysis* 49:370–374.

Kohut, H. (1972). Thoughts on narcissism and narcissistic rage. *Psychoanalytic Study of the Child* 27:360–400.

Mahler, M.S., Pine, F., and Bergman, A. (1975). *The Psychological Birth of the Human Infant.* New York: Basic Books.

Nagera, H. (1970). Children's reactions to the death of important objects: a developmental approach. *The Psychoanalytic Study of the Child* 24:360–400.

Volkan, V.D. (1981). Transference-countertransference: an examination from the point of view of internalized object relations. In *Object and Self: A Developmental Approach,* ed. S. Tuttman, C. Kaye, and M. Zimmerman, pp. 429–451.

Wolfenstein, M. (1966). How is mourning possible? *The Psychoanalytic Study of the Child* 21:93–123.

———. (1969). Loss, rage, and repetition. *The Psychoanalytic Study of the Child* 24:432–460.

3

CAN WOMEN MOURN THEIR MOTHERS?

Discussion of Meyers' Chapter, "Does Mourning Become Electra? Oedipal and Separation-Individuation Issues in a Woman's Loss of Her Mother"

Corinne Masur, Psy.D.

The death of a mother is a loss like no other, fraught as it is with the multiplicity of needs, hopes, disappointments, meanings, and memories. When this loss occurs in childhood it is particularly devastating due to the unique nature of a child's tie to his or her mother (Furman 1974). As such, maternal bereavement in childhood and the question as to whether children can complete a mourning process has generated a great deal of interest in the psychoanalytic literature in the last thirty-five years. Here Dr. Meyers asks us to turn our attention to a topic about which little has been written: the loss of the mother in adulthood, and specifically the effect of the loss of the mother on the adult woman.

Dr. Meyers uses the lens of feminine development to focus on this topic. She wonders whether there is anything universal, specific, special, or different about the loss of the mother for the woman (who has not had previous object loss in childhood) specifically as this relates to her separation-individuation process and to early identifications and disidentifications. In exploring this idea, Dr. Meyers asks what she calls a provocative question: Is classical mourning necessary for the adult woman who loses here mother? In asking this question, Dr. Meyers is suggesting that mourning, in fact, does not become Electra, while identification does. She suggests that the adult woman's self-concept and identity are strengthened, not through a painful course of grief and the work of mourning but in an identification with her mother that takes place instead of a prolonged period of mourning. This is not just a provocative suggestion, it is a radical one.

Starting with Freud (1917) and continuing through theorists, clinicians, and researchers too numerous to mention, we have been taught that mourning follows a specific, although somewhat flexible course. When this process does not occur, an "absence of grief" as originally described by Deutsch (1937) is declared and included in the category of pathological mourning. In contrast, Dr. Meyers proposes that the adult woman does not mourn in the traditional way due to the loss of the mother being more representative of a loss of the self than of a differentiated other. She suggests that the woman deals with the loss of this part of the self by a kind of "becoming mother."

THE ROLE OF IDENTIFICATION IN THE MOURNING PROCESS

In order to evaluate this idea it is necessary to understand the process of identification as it occurs in the developmental processs and to examine its role in the mourning process. Freud (1921) noted, arguably, that identification is "the earliest expression of an emotional tie to another person." More recently, identification has been defined as the process during which the self representation resembles the object representation (Volkan 1982). The purpose of identification may be to maintain a close tie to an object or its representation. When self and object are perceived as one, the self achieves relative independence insofar as it no longer needs the model to function autonomously (Volkan 1981). As such,

Corinne Masur, Psy.D.

...CTIONS ON DR. MEYERS' VIEW

...it is necessary to ask, since Dr. Meyers is describing ...which identification represents the affects usually ...with mourning but in which the identification keeps ...cts on the unconscious level, if she is describing a process ...there is the idea that there is no death, only a change ...munications and a process in which there is a fusing of the ...th the internalized object, is this to be considered healthy ...thological identification? Is she describing an "in toto" iden- ...tion effected on an imperative or emergency basis, in which ...we would suspect that a pathological mourning process is ...tually occurring, or is she describing, as she asserts, a process of ...more selective identification that results in growth and a healthy ...outcome?

What distinguishes the identification seen in Dr. Meyers' cases descriptions from other examples of healthy identificatory pro- cesses occurring at the end of the mourning process is the issue of degree. Dr. Meyers describes a more wholesale identification with mothers' abilities, values, and behavior that is to be found described elsewhere other than in the cases of "in toto" identi- fication. What she does not describe in her cases, which generally defines the "in toto" type of identification, however, is the ambivalently held aspects of the object also being identified with. In this type of total identification, depression generally follows as the mourning tuns her rage at the negative aspects of the object toward the self.

Thus, if rage toward the self and the resulting depression are not experienced by the patient, what then is the problem with Dr. Meyers' proposition that identification may obviate a more complex mourning process? In order to explore this question it is necessary to ask a few others.

In Cases 1 and 2, are Dr. Meyers' patients defending against something through their large-scale identification with their mothers? Are they attempting to avoid a more complete experi-

identification can be seen to enable the individual to feel close to important objects while simultaneously allowing independent and autonomous functioning.

In the course of normal development, the young child gradu- ally relinquishes his need for the parents' presence, substituting instead various identifications with parental abilities, functions, and roles. The pain and sadness inherent in this process is ameliorated by the gratification of growing independence, that is, by the capacity to take on these abilities, functions, and roles indepen- dently. Fueling this process is the frustration of wishing for grati- fication from an only intermittently available object. Identification with a parent's way of doing a certain task, of managing his internal state, or of defining himself in regard to gender an other roles may be transitory, as a way of carrying with oneself an internalized version of the object on the patch to truer self-definition, or it may become a more permanent part of the personality. Proceeding beyond early childhood, identification continues to play an im- portant role in development. Following the resolution of the oedipal, traditional theory has it that the child substitutes his competition with the same-sex parent with an identification with that parent in order to satisfy himself that one day he too can attain a mate just as the parent of the same sex has done. And later, during adolescence, as the teenager begins to define and consolidate his identity, identifications with parents and others are tried on and discarded or kept based on their suitability.

Just as identification is used in the process of normal devel- opment to aid in the relinquishment of the original objects, it has also long been considered an integral part of the mourning process. In 1917 Freud wrote that identification occurs when love for the lost object cannot be surrendered. He stated, however, that iden- tification may be disruptive if hate is then directed toward the internalized object as this may result in the development of melancholia or what we now refer to as depression.

In his classic study of the relatives of victims of a nightclub fire, Lindemann (1944) noted that presence of "the appearance of traits of the deceased in the behavior of the bereaved, especially symptoms seen during the last illness or behavior which may have been seen at the time of the tragedy." That is, Lindemann described a specific form of identification that occurred in acutely bereaved individuals in which they felt themselves to be ill in the same way that their lost loved one had been at the time of his death or they took on personality traits of the loved one that were characteristic of them at the time of their death. He viewed this feature of acute grief as occurring in those whose reactions "border on pathologic" (p. 142) with identification used to keep the lost loved on with the mourner in an unconscious defense against the mourning process.

Identification has also been described as one possible element in a healthy resolution to the mourning process in which there is an integration of selected qualities of the lost loved one within the personality of the bereaved. A distinction is made in the literature between selective identifications, which are, as mentioned, used for the purpose of growth and "in toto" identification, as is often seen in depression. Smith (1961) stated, "Identifications for purposes of growth are not imperative, emergency, 'in toto' internalizations. The various aspects of the objects can be experienced and specific ones can be relinquished or coordinated as enduring aspects of the self. The difference is between relatively enforced and relatively optional identifications" (p. 260).

Volkan (1981), Krupp (1965), and others have described certain types of identification as a defense against mourning. In his book, *Linking Objects and Linking Phenomena*, Volkan (1981) describes a young woman who was hospitalized for anorexia nervosa. After several months of hospital care, the nurses on her unit noted a curious pattern. Whenever the young woman's weight exceeded ninety-nine pounds, she would begin to starve herself, but once she reached a weight below ninety-nine pounds she would eat quite normally again. It was not until Volkan began to treat this young woman in a psychoanalytic psychotherapy that the symbolic meaning of the number ninety-nine became

clear. The young wo
earlier following t
robust man, he ha
Protected from seeing
funeral that his granddau
As she stood by his casket s
have weighed more than nine
death. Upon hearing this the gr
until the meaning of her relentless i
nine pounds was discovered to be an
with her deceased grandfather, and a wa,
that the patient was able to experience her
loss, to mourn, to give up her identification,
normally again.

Similarly, Krupp (1965) discussed the importa
fication following object loss, citing a number of cas
patients identified strongly with a lost loved one, particu
their personality and the symptoms experienced in their last
Krupp refers to what he terms "identification symptoms" (p.
defining these as unconscious mechanisms for containing the pain
affects associated with the loss. In one case Krupp proposed that
his patient's identification with his dead father represented yearning for the father, a denial that the father was permanently lost,
and rage at being deserted, all experienced on the unconscious
level. Yearning, sadness, and rage are the affects classically associated
with the mourning process, and they are exactly those which Dr.
Meyers suggests may not be present in the adult woman. Furthermore, Krupp, like Deutsch and others commented that a lack of
both grief and significant depressive affect following the loss of a
close loved one indicates pathology. He suggested that when
identification is excessive and persistent it has an unconscious
fantasy value that translates into the notion that there is no death,
only a change in communication. The mourner attempts to recover the lost object by reactivation of old introjects and a fusing
of the self with the internalized object.

At this poin
a process
associated
these aff
in whic
in com
self w
or p
tifi
ca
a

encing of the painful affects of grief and mourning? This is one possibility. Alternatively, is it possible that they are defending against the furthering of the separation-individuation process begun so long ago and that they have reasons to do so beyond the particular nature of feminine development? In these two case examples one must wonder if Dr. Meyers is describing women who are as well separated as she originally proposed. Both chose to go into their mothers' professions, to remain in the same city with mother, and in Case 2 to continue to please mother and to remain subservient to her. These are not choices that can be considered typical of the well-separated adult woman. Is it possible that because these women were not as well separated from their mothers as they might have been that they had not traversed the first two prototypical periods of mourning (rapprochment and adolescence) optimally and thus were not well disposed to manage the mourning process and to decathect from mother—as an external or an internal object—in an optimal fashion?

During the rapprochment period the little girl may not experience the opportunity to express the full force of her hostility toward mother, including her wish to leave mother, to be different from mother, and to feel differently than mother, due in some degree to the particular process of feminine development. However is it not possible that this occurs to a greater extent because she exists in a dyad with a powerfully controlling mother (as the mothers in Cases 1 and 2) or a mother who is narcissistically preoccupied, depressed, or unable to tolerate her daughter's hostility, rage, and efforts toward separation for any number of other reasons? In such cases, the girl may be left following the rapprochment period with the need to subjugate her own needs, desires, and authentic feelings to inhibition and repression in order to please the external mother and to maintain a positively held internal image of the mother. As such, the girl is limited in her ability to engage in the prototypic mourning process referred to by Dr. Meyers because she is actually not as fully able to relinquish the symbiotic object as she might be. Similarly, in normal adolescence, there is "disengagement of libidinal and aggressive cathexes from the internalized love and hate objects: (Blos 1979, p. 179). This is the second prototypical mourning mentioned by Dr. Meyers and again it is possible that in women who do not engage in the adolescent process as fully as they might due to either real difficulty negotiating the process with a highly controlling, fragile, or otherwise disturbed mother or a reluctance to disengage from the positively held internalized image of the mother, it can be expected that there will be both limitations in the experiencing and expression of the woman's authentic and unique self and difficulties later on in attempting further disengagement from mother at the time of mother's death, that is, to participate in the work of mourning.

Is it thus reasonable to say, as an alternative to Dr. Meyers' hypothesis, that in a *subset* of adult women who have not experienced early object loss per se and who have also not been able to separate optimally from their mothers that identification with mother at the time of her death might both be adaptive and defensive? That is, that while "becoming mother" might be the best resolution possible for them following mother's death, it may also represent a defense against experiencing both the reality of their loss and the painful feelings associated with that loss. And following from this, is it reasonable to then say that for the larger population of more optimally separated women, mourning is still the rule? But what is lost for the women who identify rather than mourn? It can be suggested that while identification may be, as stated, the best adaptation possible for them at this time, they forfeit an experiencing of their true and passionate feelings both about their mothers and the loss of their mothers as well as a sense of themselves as independent, authentic, and unique individuals.

Alternatively, I wonder if perhaps a more classical process of mourning might yet be in store even for Dr. Meyers' two patients and women like them. It is true that in the Eugene O'Neill play, *Mourning Becomes Electra*, to which Dr. Meyers' title refers, O'Neill's main character, Lavinia, does take on the manner and appearance of mother after her mother's death. As O'Neill states, "Lavinia appears in the doorway. . . In the lighted room, the change in her is strikingly apparent. At first glance, one would mistake her for her mother as she appeared in the First Act. . . She seems a mature woman, sure of her feminine attractiveness. Her brown-gold hair is arranged as her mother's had been. Her green dress is like a copy of her mother's . . ." (p. 1016). But this is not the end of the story. Following a subsequent loss, that of her brother, Lavinia's guilt, rage, and depression surface; she reverts to her former rigid, asexual, hostile self, and she enters a period of prolonged mourning. Is it possible that what seems like a permanent identification with mother in some adult women may in time, perhaps with the provocation of another loss, give way to a traditional mourning process followed by the development of a more consolidated and authentic sense of a unique self?

CONCLUSION

I would like to make one final point. At the end of her paper, Dr. Meyers questions the work of Drs. Robert and Erna Furman in terms of their analytic technique with bereaved children and their suggestions as to the manner in which to handle the topic of death with non-bereaved children. In the literature on early childhood bereavement, the Furmans' work stands alone in its sensitivity and depth. They propose a developmental sequence to the mourning process and answer the old debate as to whether children can mourn by stating that after the development of object constancy the young child does indeed have the capacity to mourn given adequate care, external support, and modeling of the affects of grief. At no point do the Furmans suggest teaching children about the phases of mourning or pointing out dead insects or animals. Rather, they suggest that allowing the young child to ask questions about what he experiences in the natural environment and answering these questions with sensitivity prepares the child for later loss far better than avoiding the subject of death in an attempt to "protect the child."Vis-à-vis the treatment of childhood bereavement, Dr. Meyers suggests that the Furmans may create a traumatic effect in their young patients by attempting to bring out "what is not there."At first this seeming non sequitor in Dr. Meyers paper was perplexing. How did this point relate to the previously discussed material? Finally it became apparent that what Dr. Meyers objects to in the Furmans work relates to her formulation. If Dr. Meyers' first two patients can identify with mother as the best possible solution to their loss, that is, if they cannot experience the affects associated with grief and do the work of mourning, then interpretation of an underlying grief or mourning process might indeed be traumatic as Dr. Meyers fears that it is when the Furmans do this with their young patients. On the other hand, if Dr. Meyers' patients might be able to experience a more affectively expressive mourning process, if their identification with mother is, in face, defensive then it might be beneficial rather than nonempathic to attempt to access the unconscious sadness, yearning, rage, and guilt, in order to allow them to more fully separate from mother and to develop a more authentic sense of their unique selves as women. The difference between the Furmans and Dr. Meyers is, I think, that the Furmans believe that their young patients can mourn. Dr. Meyers does not believe that of some of her adult women patients.

REFERENCES

Blos, P. (1979). *The Adolescent Passage*. New York: International Universities Press.

Deutsch, H. (1937). The absence of grief. *Psychoanalytic Quarterly* 6:12–22.

Freud, S. (1917). Mourning and melancholia. *Standard Edition* 14:237–258.

————. (1921). Group psychology and the analysis of the ego. *Standard Edition* 18:67–144.

Furman, E. (1974). *A Child's Parent Dies*. New Haven, CT: Yale University Press.

Krupp, G. (1965). Identification as a defence against anxiety in coping with loss. *International Journal of Psycho-Analysis* 46:303–314.

Lindemann, E. (1944). Symptomatology and management of acute grief. *American Journal of Psychiatry* 101:141:148.

O'Neill, E. (1988). *Complete Plays: 1920–1931*. New York: Literary Classics of the United States.

Smith, J.H. (1971). Identificatory styles in depression and grief. *International Journal of Psycho-Analysis* 52:259–266.

Volkan, V.D. (1981). *Linking Objects and Linking Phenomena*. New York: International Universities, Press, Inc.

DEFENSES EVOKED BY EARLY CHILDHOOD LOSS: THEIR IMPACT ON LIFE-SPAN DEVELOPMENT

Calvin F. Settlage, M.D.

identification can be seen to enable the individual to feel close to important objects while simultaneously allowing independent and autonomous functioning.

In the course of normal development, the young child gradually relinquishes his need for the parents' presence, substituting instead various identifications with parental abilities, functions, and roles. The pain and sadness inherent in this process is ameliorated by the gratification of growing independence, that is, by the capacity to take on these abilities, functions, and roles independently. Fueling this process is the frustration of wishing for gratification from an only intermittently available object. Identification with a parent's way of doing a certain task, of managing his internal state, or of defining himself in regard to gender an other roles may be transitory, as a way of carrying with oneself an internalized version of the object on the patch to truer self-definition, or it may become a more permanent part of the personality. Proceeding beyond early childhood, identification continues to play an important role in development. Following the resolution of the oedipal, traditional theory has it that the child substitutes his competition with the same-sex parent with an identification with that parent in order to satisfy himself that one day he too can attain a mate just as the parent of the same sex has done. And later, during adolescence, as the teenager begins to define and consolidate his identity, identifications with parents and others are tried on and discarded or kept based on their suitability.

Just as identification is used in the process of normal development to aid in the relinquishment of the original objects, it has also long been considered an integral part of the mourning process. In 1917 Freud wrote that identification occurs when love for the lost object cannot be surrendered. He stated, however, that identification may be disruptive if hate is then directed toward the internalized object as this may result in the development of melancholia or what we now refer to as depression.

In his classic study of the relatives of victims of a nightclub fire, Lindemann (1944) noted that presence of "the appearance of traits of the deceased in the behavior of the bereaved, especially symptoms seen during the last illness or behavior which may have been seen at the time of the tragedy." That is, Lindemann described a specific form of identification that occurred in acutely bereaved individuals in which they felt themselves to be ill in the same way that their lost loved one had been at the time of his death or they took on personality traits of the loved one that were characteristic of them at the time of their death. He viewed this feature of acute grief as occurring in those whose reactions "border on pathologic" (p. 142) with identification used to keep the lost loved on with the mourner in an unconscious defense against the mourning process.

Identification has also been described as one possible element in a healthy resolution to the mourning process in which there is an integration of selected qualities of the lost loved one within the personality of the bereaved. A distinction is made in the literature between selective identifications, which are, as mentioned, used for the purpose of growth and "in toto" identification, as is often seen in depression. Smith (1961) stated, "Identifications for purposes of growth are not imperative, emergency, 'in toto' internalizations. The various aspects of the objects can be experienced and specific ones can be relinquished or coordinated as enduring aspects of the self. The difference is between relatively enforced and relatively optional identifications" (p. 260).

Volkan (1981), Krupp (1965), and others have described certain types of identification as a defense against mourning. In his book, *Linking Objects and Linking Phenomena*, Volkan (1981) describes a young woman who was hospitalized for anorexia nervosa. After several months of hospital care, the nurses on her unit noted a curious pattern. Whenever the young woman's weight exceeded ninety-nine pounds, she would begin to starve herself, but once she reached a weight below ninety-nine pounds she would eat quite normally again. It was not until Volkan began to treat this young woman in a psychoanalytic psychotherapy that the symbolic meaning of the number ninety-nine became clear. The young woman's illness had commenced three years earlier following the death of her beloved grandfather. Once a robust man, he had fallen ill and had quickly wasted away. Protected from seeing him while he was ill, it was not until his funeral that his granddaughter saw how thin he had become. As she stood by his casket someone remarked that he could not have weighed more than ninety-nine pounds at the time of his death. Upon hearing this the granddaughter fainted. It was not until the meaning of her relentless insistence on weighing ninety-nine pounds was discovered to be an unconscious identification with her deceased grandfather, and a way to keep him with her, that the patient was able to experience her deep sadness over his loss, to mourn, to give up her identification, and to begin to eat normally again.

Similarly, Krupp (1965) discussed the importance of identification following object loss, citing a number of cases in which patients identified strongly with a lost loved one, particularly with their personality and the symptoms experienced in their last illness. Krupp refers to what he terms "identification symptoms" (p. 306) defining these as unconscious mechanisms for containing the painful affects associated with the loss. In one case Krupp proposed that his patient's identification with his dead father represented yearning for the father, a denial that the father was permanently lost, and rage at being deserted, all experienced on the unconscious level. Yearning, sadness, and rage are the affects classically associated with the mourning process, and they are exactly those which Dr. Meyers suggests may not be present in the adult woman. Furthermore, Krupp, like Deutsch and others commented that a lack of both grief and significant depressive affect following the loss of a close loved one indicates pathology. He suggested that when identification is excessive and persistent it has an unconscious fantasy value that translates into the notion that there is no death, only a change in communication. The mourner attempts to recover the lost object by reactivation of old introjects and a fusing of the self with the internalized object.

REFLECTIONS ON DR. MEYERS' VIEW

At this point it is necessary to ask, since Dr. Meyers is describing a process in which identification represents the affects usually associated with mourning but in which the identification keeps these affects on the unconscious level, if she is describing a process in which there is the idea that there is no death, only a change in communications and a process in which there is a fusing of the self with the internalized object, is this to be considered healthy or pathological identification? Is she describing an "in toto" identification effected on an imperative or emergency basis, in which case we would suspect that a pathological mourning process is actually occurring, or is she describing, as she asserts, a process of more selective identification that results in growth and a healthy outcome?

What distinguishes the identification seen in Dr. Meyers' cases descriptions from other examples of healthy identificatory processes occurring at the end of the mourning process is the issue of degree. Dr. Meyers describes a more wholesale identification with mothers' abilities, values, and behavior that is to be found described elsewhere other than in the cases of "in toto" identification. What she does not describe in her cases, which generally defines the "in toto" type of identification, however, is the ambivalently held aspects of the object also being identified with. In this type of total identification, depression generally follows as the mourning tuns her rage at the negative aspects of the object toward the self.

Thus, if rage toward the self and the resulting depression are not experienced by the patient, what then is the problem with Dr. Meyers' proposition that identification may obviate a more complex mourning process? In order to explore this question it is necessary to ask a few others.

In Cases 1 and 2, are Dr. Meyers' patients defending against something through their large-scale identification with their mothers? Are they attempting to avoid a more complete experiencing of the painful affects of grief and mourning? This is one possibility. Alternatively, is it possible that they are defending against the furthering of the separation-individuation process begun so long ago and that they have reasons to do so beyond the particular nature of feminine development? In these two case examples one must wonder if Dr. Meyers is describing women who are as well separated as she originally proposed. Both chose to go into their mothers' professions, to remain in the same city with mother, and in Case 2 to continue to please mother and to remain subservient to her. These are not choices that can be considered typical of the well-separated adult woman. Is it possible that because these women were not as well separated from their mothers as they might have been that they had not traversed the first two prototypical periods of mourning (rapprochment and adolescence) optimally and thus were not well disposed to manage the mourning process and to decathect from mother—as an external or an internal object—in an optimal fashion?

During the rapprochment period the little girl may not experience the opportunity to express the full force of her hostility toward mother, including her wish to leave mother, to be different from mother, and to feel differently than mother, due in some degree to the particular process of feminine development. However is it not possible that this occurs to a greater extent because she exists in a dyad with a powerfully controlling mother (as the mothers in Cases 1 and 2) or a mother who is narcissistically preoccupied, depressed, or unable to tolerate her daughter's hostility, rage, and efforts toward separation for any number of other reasons? In such cases, the girl may be left following the rapprochment period with the need to subjugate her own needs, desires, and authentic feelings to inhibition and repression in order to please the external mother and to maintain a positively held internal image of the mother. As such, the girl is limited in her ability to engage in the prototypic mourning process referred to by Dr. Meyers because she is actually not as fully able to relinquish the symbiotic object as she might be. Similarly, in normal adolescence, there is "disengagement of libidinal and aggressive cathexes from the internalized love and hate objects: (Blos 1979, p. 179). This is the second prototypical mourning mentioned by Dr. Meyers and again it is possible that in women who do not engage in the adolescent process as fully as they might due to either real difficulty negotiating the process with a highly controlling, fragile, or otherwise disturbed mother or a reluctance to disengage from the positively held internalized image of the mother, it can be expected that there will be both limitations in the experiencing and expression of the woman's authentic and unique self and difficulties later on in attempting further disengagement from mother at the time of mother's death, that is, to participate in the work of mourning.

Is it thus reasonable to say, as an alternative to Dr. Meyers' hypothesis, that in a *subset* of adult women who have not experienced early object loss per se and who have also not been able to separate optimally from their mothers that identification with mother at the time of her death might both be adaptive and defensive? That is, that while "becoming mother" might be the best resolution possible for them following mother's death, it may also represent a defense against experiencing both the reality of their loss and the painful feelings associated with that loss. And following from this, is it reasonable to then say that for the larger population of more optimally separated women, mourning is still the rule? But what is lost for the women who identify rather than mourn? It can be suggested that while identification may be, as stated, the best adaptation possible for them at this time, they forfeit an experiencing of their true and passionate feelings both about their mothers and the loss of their mothers as well as a sense of themselves as independent, authentic, and unique individuals.

Alternatively, I wonder if perhaps a more classical process of mourning might yet be in store even for Dr. Meyers' two patients and women like them. It is true that in the Eugene O'Neill play, *Mourning Becomes Electra*, to which Dr. Meyers' title refers, O'Neill's main character, Lavinia, does take on the manner and appearance of mother after her mother's death. As O'Neill states, "Lavinia appears in the doorway. . . In the lighted room, the change in her is strikingly apparent. At first glance, one would mistake her for her mother as she appeared in the First Act. . . She seems a mature woman, sure of her feminine attractiveness. Her brown-gold hair is arranged as her mother's had been. Her green dress is like a copy of her mother's . . ." (p. 1016). But this is not the end of the story. Following a subsequent loss, that of her brother, Lavinia's guilt, rage, and depression surface; she reverts to her former rigid, asexual, hostile self, and she enters a period of prolonged mourning. Is it possible that what seems like a permanent identification with mother in some adult women may in time, perhaps with the provocation of another loss, give way to a traditional mourning process followed by the development of a more consolidated and authentic sense of a unique self?

CONCLUSION

I would like to make one final point. At the end of her paper, Dr. Meyers questions the work of Drs. Robert and Erna Furman in terms of their analytic technique with bereaved children and their suggestions as to the manner in which to handle the topic of death with non-bereaved children. In the literature on early childhood bereavement, the Furmans' work stands alone in its sensitivity and depth. They propose a developmental sequence to the mourning process and answer the old debate as to whether children can mourn by stating that after the development of object constancy the young child does indeed have the capacity to mourn given adequate care, external support, and modeling of the affects of grief. At no point do the Furmans suggest teaching children about the phases of mourning or pointing out dead insects or animals. Rather, they suggest that allowing the young child to ask questions about what he experiences in the natural environment and answering these questions with sensitivity prepares the child for later loss far better than avoiding the subject of death in an attempt to "protect the child." Vis-à-vis the treatment of childhood bereavement, Dr. Meyers suggests that the Furmans may create a traumatic effect in their young patients by attempting to bring out "what is not there." At first this seeming non sequitor in Dr. Meyers paper was perplexing. How did this point relate to the previously discussed material? Finally it became apparent that what Dr. Meyers objects to in the Furmans work relates to her formulation. If Dr. Meyers' first two patients can identify with mother as the best possible solution to their loss, that is, if they cannot experience the affects associated with grief and do the work of mourning, then interpretation of an underlying grief or mourning process might indeed be traumatic as Dr. Meyers fears that it is when the Furmans do this with their young patients. On the other hand, if Dr. Meyers' patients might be able to experience a more affectively expressive mourning process, if their identification with mother is, in face, defensive then it might be beneficial rather than nonempathic to attempt to access the unconscious sadness, yearning, rage, and guilt, in order to allow them to more fully separate from mother and to develop a more authentic sense of their unique selves as women. The difference between the Furmans and Dr. Meyers is, I think, that the Furmans believe that their young patients can mourn. Dr. Meyers does not believe that of some of her adult women patients.

REFERENCES

Blos, P. (1979). *The Adolescent Passage.* New York: International Universities Press.

Deutsch, H. (1937). The absence of grief. *Psychoanalytic Quarterly* 6:12–22.

Freud, S. (1917). Mourning and melancholia. *Standard Edition* 14:237–258.

———. (1921). Group psychology and the analysis of the ego. *Standard Edition* 18:67–144.

Furman, E. (1974). *A Child's Parent Dies.* New Haven, CT: Yale University Press.

Krupp, G. (1965). Identification as a defence against anxiety in coping with loss. *International Journal of Psycho-Analysis* 46:303–314.

Lindemann, E. (1944). Symptomatology and management of acute grief. *American Journal of Psychiatry* 101:141:148.

O'Neill, E. (1988). *Complete Plays: 1920–1931*. New York: Literary Classics of the United States.

Smith, J.H. (1971). Identificatory styles in depression and grief. *International Journal of Psycho-Analysis* 52:259–266.

Volkan, V.D. (1981). *Linking Objects and Linking Phenomena*. New York: International Universities, Press, Inc.

DEFENSES EVOKED BY EARLY CHILDHOOD LOSS: THEIR IMPACT ON LIFE-SPAN DEVELOPMENT

Calvin F. Settlage, M.D.

Separation–individuation theory stresses the importance of the mother's libidinal availability to the child in support of the child's psychological development (Mahler, Pine, and Bergman 1975). *Libidinal* refers to the developmentally crucial love of the mother for her child. In infant development, *libidinal availability* can be read equally well as *emotional availability*. My presentation will focus first on libidinal loss of relationship with the mother as a normal and a pathogenic experience in early childhood, and second on the relationship of pathological childhood loss to the adult capacity to mourn the actual loss of a loved one. Loss of relationship with the mother, the primary love object in Freud's terms, entails either the real or imagined *threat of loss* or *actual loss* of love. My motivation for this discussion of libidinal loss and its effects, and for illustration of the technique for the treatment of the resulting psychopathology arises from involvement in developmental research and from clinical experience.

The impact of libidinal loss on development was observed

in studies of child–parent interaction during the rapprochement subphase of separation-individuation. The research included the discovery, conceptualization, and cross-cultural application of the appeal cycle (Settlage, Rosenthal et al. 1990; Settlage, Bemesderfer et al. 1991; Okimoto, Settlage et al. 2001). One study observed mother-child and father-child interaction with the same child (Settlage, Silver et al. 1993). Not only mothers but fathers, mother-surrogates, and others contribute importantly to infant care and development. Because the initial involvement of the infant is usually with the mother, I will use the word *mother* instead of the more broadly applicable term *caregiver*.

In the experimental situation of the research, the circumstance of the mother and child being alone together is intruded upon by a telephone call to the mother and then an interview with the mother in the child's presence. These intrusions created a separation in the child–parent relationship and caused the child to experience libidinal loss. Although the observational situation included a brief physical separation of child and parent, as in attachment theory research (Ainsworth and Wittig 1969), it was libidinal separation that permitted the discovery of the appeal cycle. An important feature of libidinal separation, in contrast to physical separation, is that the child and the parent being in each other's presence furthers communication and restitution of the developmental relationship in the immediate context of its disruption. These phenomena are evident in the four phases of the appeal cycle: *adaptation* to the mother's diminished availability, *distress* as the attentuated relationship continues, *appeal* to the mother for libidinal contact and relief of the distress, and a resulting *interaction* that restores the disrupted relationship and the child's emotional equilibrium.

My motivating clinical experience involved therapeutic work with child and adult patients who suffered libidinal loss in early childhood. Developmental arrest often is associated with significant libidinal loss and the related psychopathology. The technique therefore includes the facilitation of the natural tendency to resume development as well as the resolution of pathology through the analysis of defenses and the interpretation of transference. From psychoanalytic observation of the process of psychological change and growth in patients ranging in age from very young to very old, I believe that an important factor in the resumption of development is the patient's use of the analyst as a developmental object as well as a transference object (Settlage 1996, p. 556). This concept is illustrated in the presented case material and discussed in *CLOSING COMMENTS*.

I will be referring to three cases. In two of the patients— a boy, Ira, who was 3½ years old at the beginning of treatment and a woman, Ilana, who was 28—early loss caused intractable separation anxiety. The third patient, Kate, suffered both libidinal loss in early childhood and the actual loss at age 63 of her husband who died in a tragic automobile accident. Her childhood loss had been dealt with, seemingly effectively, in a completed analysis conducted during her adult years.

The patients with intractable separation anxiety experienced the physical loss of me when I moved from California to Arkansas four years ago during their treatment. My leaving these patients introduced a unique and undesirable variable into their treatment, one that held the potential of being experienced as a reinforcing repetition of the trauma of loss. But my loss was not a total loss. With the aim of completing their analyses, I offered and undertook telephone work with a number of my patients. I meet with these patients twice a year in California in order to renew and affirm our in-person relationship. I met several times with Ira during return visits to California and I am working by telephone with Ilana. This work after the separation provided the opportunity to observe their reaction to my leaving while continuing to analyze the effect of the early childhood separations. Resuming analytic work by phone with Kate allowed me to observe the relationship between her defensive responses to childhood loss and her adult capacity to mourn the loss of her husband.

In the phone work with Ilana, I had the unique experience

of her becoming drowsy and falling asleep while she was in her
bed and talking to me on the phone. This suggested the reenactment of the infantile experience of separation brought about
by the infant's falling asleep. From Ilana's reporting on the treatment, I knew that her mother was inconsistently available during
the patient's early childhood. By inference, I wondered whether
Ilana had experienced libidinal loss in the sleep situation of her
infancy. Thinking about this possibility prompted me to survey the
evidence for affective and defensive reaction to libidinal loss during
the preverbal period of postnatal development.

THE LEGACY OF EVOLUTION

Evolution accounts for human nature and the human condition.
The evolutionary move of the human species was away from
survival relying on inherited, instinctive patterns of behavior to
survival based on a prolonged dependency safeguarded by the
parent (Parens and Saul 1971). Mahler, et al. observed that the
equipment and functions for self-preservation are atrophied in
the human infant and are supplanted by the emotional rapport of
the mother's nurturant care in a kind of social symbiosis (1968;
Mahler, Pine, and Bergman 1975). Freud (1926, p. 155) noted that
the infant's biological situation of helplessness and dependency
established the earliest circumstance of danger and created the
need to be loved, which accompanies the child through the rest
of its life. Spitz (1963) postulated that the human foetus and
newborn infant have a built-in, organismic sense of vital unity
with the mother. This innate sense makes the newborn infant turn
toward the mother in a survival-serving move. The emotional
nurturance of love, empathy, caring, and relatedness is as vital for
humans as are physical and physiological nurturance. Evolution
embedded love into human nature and human development (Lear
1990, J. Novick and K. Novick 2000).

Emotional nurturance in its various forms is the vehicle for ontogenetic or individual development as it recapitulates the phylogenetic development of the species. Phylogenetic development involved evolutionary advances from lower levels of organization to the high levels of organization represented by the complex emotional and mental functioning of the human being. At its outset, individual development is achieved within the mother–infant interaction. This interaction facilitates development of the unfolding capacities of consciousness, memory, language, intelligence, thought, creativity, and the ability to learn from experience. Good interactive experience with the mother is internalized and contributes to the formation of a sound sense of self and self-regulatory mental structure.

The intimate closeness of the symbiotic beginning of post-natal life and the sequential unfolding of inherited capacities require and actuate separation–individuation. In Mahler's conceptualization, separation is the necessary concomitant of the biologically-predetermined thrust of individuation (Mahler et al. 1975). Separation–individuation implements the progressive, hierarchical, developmental moves of individuation and the corresponding moves of separation. Each step in individuation entails relinquishment of a dependency tie to the mother. The ongoing, step–wise internalization of experience with the mother enables tolerance of separation without excessive anxiety and the acceptance of separateness. As Mahler cogently conceived, the mental representation of experience with the mother in the child's object and self constancy structures makes the mother constantly available to the child in the internal world of the child (ibid).

The Neurobiological and Experiential Bases
of Human Development

Infantile affects are the precursors of the more complex emotions. The central nervous system is so constructed that all experience is affective (Emde 1983, p. 173). The infant's affects are pre-adapted for human interaction (Emde 1980, Stern 1985). Through phylogenesis, the earliest human affects and anxieties are innate and automatic reactions (Emde 1983). The capacity to anticipate danger also is biologically innate (Schur 1966, Hall 1999). The infant's first communications to the mother are nonverbal gestures based on early collations of sensations from within the body (Spitz 1964). These gathered-together sensations are expressed in facial and vocal gestures that convey pleasure, interest, surprise, fear, distress, anger, sadness, and disgust (Emde 1983). An important element in successful mother–infant communication is the ability to tune in on each other's affective and emotional states. This exchange is termed *primary intersubjectivity* (Trevarthen 1979).

Mutual mother–infant regulatory patterns can be observed as early as age 10 days (Sander 1962). Nuanced, experience-linked, affective responses develop in the infant by $3^1/2$ months (Pine 1986). Because of biological preadaptation, the infant quickly attunes to the world, becomes differentially responsive, and learns from experience (Pine 1986). Affective mother–infant interaction is "the trail breaker" for development (Spitz 1965, p. 140).

Neuropsychological research has complemented and given credence to the psychoanalytic understanding of infant development. Findings from this research demonstrate that biologically provided potentials and postnatal experience are mutually influential. Although operating under set instructions from heredity, brain development is not tightly programmed. The brain develops through a Darwinian, neural selection process that favors adaptation (Edelman 1992). "Selection not only guarantees a common pattern in a species but also results in *individual* diversity at the highest level of the finest neural networks (p. 64). This linkage between brain development and adaptive development links biological and psychological processes.

The same linkage has been defined by research on the relationship between neurobiological studies of the developing brain and psychological studies of mother–infant interaction. The infant's affective interactions with the mother influence the postnatal maturation of the brain structures that will regulate future social and emotional functioning (Schore 1994). Developmental neuroscience ascribes the mediation of this functioning to the orbitofrontal cortex and its interconnections with subcortical systems. The subcortical limbic system is the locus of affective functioning. This mediation has been confirmed by the use of the technically advanced imaging tools of magnetic resonance imaging (MRI) and positron emission tomography (PET). These techniques enable the researcher to observe the location in neural pathways of activity in the brain associated with emotional and mental states such as fear, worry, and obsessive preoccupation.

Neurophysiological evidence indicates that preverbal affective experience is recorded in the limbic structures of the right hemisphere of the brain (Schore 1994). Research in molecular biology indicates that anxiety originates from unconsciously recorded infantile experience (Kandel 1983, 1999). In addition, cognitive science has contributed the concept of procedural memory of preverbal experience (Clyman 1992). Antedating evocative memory, procedural memory cannot be consciously recalled. Yet, procedural memory is not subject to infantile amnesia (Clyman 1991).

Drawing on his discovery that repression submerges but does not eradicate memory, seventy years ago Freud postulated that nothing once formed in mental life can perish. Everything is somehow preserved and in suitable circumstances can be brought back to light (Freud 1930, p. 69). Contemporary brain studies elucidating the locus of memory do lend support to Freud's hypothesis. However, the characterization of brain development in infancy as a dynamic, selectional process involving competition between populations of neurons means that some populations of neurons are selected and others are not and die out (Edelman 1992, p. 64). Assuming that memory was a function of the neurons that die out, memory of some early experience would perish.

Since preverbal experience is stored, it can be expressed and potentially brought into conscious awareness through creative acts such as writing poetry (Settlage 1996, p. 559) and in the dreams,

screen memories, and transference manifestations of analytic patients (Kramer 1980, P. Kernberg 1980, Akhtar 1991). If a preverbal infant can experience libidinal loss while falling asleep in the
physical but not the emotional presence of the mother, as is
suggested by the case of Ilana, this experience can be recovered
through its reenactment in the transference to the analyst.

A major biobehavioral shift occurs at about age 12 months.
It involves synthesizing epigenetic advances in cognitive, motor,
and affective functions (Schore 1994). As will be noted under *The
Infant's Experience of Loss* and *The Emergence of Defenses,* this shift
links neurobiological development and the psychoanalytic theory
of development in two specific instances. It suggests a neurobiological basis for the advent of the experience of separation and
libidinal loss and for the emergence of the capacity for defense.
Freud's (1920, p. 60) expectation that biology would in the future
provide information affirming or disaffirming psychoanalytic
hypotheses is being fulfilled.

THE INFANT'S EXPERIENCE OF LOSS

Establishment of the symbiotic, affective relationship is a precondition for the experience of loss (Emde 1980). The infant's experience of loss is attributed to the gradual development of a sense
of separateness from the symbiotic partner. The infant's earliest
reaction to separation is placed at 2 to 4 months of age. Various
observers of infant development describe this agreed-upon finding
in different ways:

- Strong evidence of displeasure at separation (Provence and
  Lipton 1962).
- Negative emotion upon loss of the human being (Decarie
  1965).
- A reaction of unpleasure and crying when left by the adult
  partner (Spitz 1946).

• A fleeting sense of loss (Escalona 1968).

Anxiety as a reaction to loss appears later than the infant's first reaction to separation, at about 6 months of age. Severe or extended libidinal loss and actual loss of the mother at this age are thought to be experienced at an organismic level as a threat to survival (Spitz 1946). This threat appears to evoke *annihilation anxiety*. If not relieved, annihilation anxiety is followed by apathy and a physical decline having an aura of death. Annihilation anxiety is manifested in failure-to-thrive, in anaclitic depression, and in marasmus (Spitz 1946). Marasmus can result in death.

Eight months anxiety is the infant's reaction to sensing that the mother is a separate entity. Occurring at about 9 months, *stranger anxiety* is a reaction to sensing that the stranger is not mother. At age 12 months, prefrontal, cortical circuits and their connections with the affective limbic system are activated (Schore 1994). This advance in brain development and the stress of separation appear to be mutually influential. The result is a cognitively-heightened awareness of separateness that lies between the earlier levels of awareness and the definitive awareness of separateness that Mahler places at 15 to 16 months of age (Mahler et al. 1975). The establishment of object permanency at about 18 months (Piaget 1954) is essential for evocative memory and the child's full realization that the mother is a separate object from the child. The anxiety associated with the intermediate awareness of separateness at the beginning of the second year of life presages the clear-cut, heightened separation anxiety that triggers the rapprochement crisis at about 18 months of age (Mahler et al. 1975).

THE EMERGENCE OF DEFENSES

Affective reactions to loss necessarily precede the defensive responses that they evoke. The described biobehavioral shift at 12 months of age includes the maturation of the forebrain inhibitory systems that introduce cortical control of subcortical affects (ibid). This neurobiological advance would appear to support the psychoanalytic concept of defense and suggest the time of emergence of defense.

Defenses operate at an unconscious level at the behest of the unconscious part of the ego. Freud (1937, p. 227) said that repression is a defense mechanism employed by the immature, feeble ego. He allowed, though, for the possibility that the mental apparatus makes use of different methods of defense prior to its "sharp cleavage" into id and ego (Freud 1926, p. 164). This possibility appears to be affirmed by Fraiberg's (1982) studies of infants who were suffering grave deficiencies in object relations. She saw the primitive defensive behaviors of these infants as extreme reactions to the damaging influence of the mother and as analogous to the fight–flight behaviors of other animals. She termed these reactive defensive behaviors avoidance, freezing, and fighting. The later emerging *ego defenses* are less primitive than these *behavioral defenses*. Still, the fact that defenses are evoked in early infancy and operate unconsciously under a rudimentary ego (Spitz 1965) does suggest that they are the human equivalent of the instinctive *fight–flight* behaviors of other animals.

Adaptation and defense have common roots (Mahler and McDevitt 1968). Defenses are first employed in the service of adaptation to the external world. Because of dependence on the mother for protection and survival, the infant's initial adaptation is to the maternal world. The infant's capacity for postnatal bonding includes an innate sensitivity to the strength of the affective tie to the mother. Defenses are evoked in the infant when either the mother's behavior or the infant's behavior threaten this tie. In the developing infant, relationship-threatening affects and urges are repressed, notably anger and aggression. The blockage of expression of affects can evoke denial of the inadequacy of the parenting and force the precocious development of coping capabilities (Blos 2000). But the apparently strong ego is in fact fragile and only pseudo–mature (ibid).

Freud (1923) insightfully perceived that repression transformed danger in the infant's parental world into danger in the infant's internal world. Repression submerges urges and feelings that are met by parental disapproval. Freud's concept of the *dynamic unconscious* recognized that continued avoidance of conflict with the parents requires the active maintenance of repressive control over the relationship-threatening feelings. In this regard, Anna Freud (1946, p. 45) noted that "defense is the earliest representative of the dynamic standpoint in psychoanalytic theory." The defenses discussed by Anna Freud are repression, regression, reaction-formation, isolation, displacement, undoing, introjection, identification, projection, turning against the self, denial, reversal, intellectualization, and sublimation. My discussion of pathogenesis in infancy and early childhood is focused on the defense of repression and the defense of splitting. Splitting is not among the defenses discussed by Anna Freud. Its delineation awaited direct observation of infant development (Mahler 1971) and clinical work with borderline personality disorders (Kernberg 1975).

PREOEDIPAL PATHOGENESIS AND PSYCHOPATHOLOGY[1]

Ironically, human postnatal development accounts for both the high adaptive capability of the human species and for the species-specific vulnerability to emotional illness. The adaptive capability arises from the extraordinary achievements of postnatal development. The vulnerability lies in the fact that development can be impaired as well as enhanced by environmental influence. The

---

[1]Although the individual time-table for development is variable, it is generally agreed that oedipal development begins at about age three years. The term *preoedipal* refers essentially to the first three years of life.

following elements constitute the matrix of preoedipal pathogenesis and psychopathology:

- The prolonged period of postnatal development requiring suitable child–parent interaction.
- The infant's dependency on the mother for survival.
- The related innate sensitivity to loss of relationship.
- The built-in defensive response to the threat of loss.
- The dynamic functioning of the unconscious mind.

The Developmental Dilemma

An instrumental factor in preoedipal pathogenesis is the developmental dilemma of the human infant. The infant develops in a situation requiring the maintenance of an ongoing stable, supportive relationship with the mother. Yet the child's developmental destiny is to individuate and separate from this mother. The parental role in fulfillment of the child's development is to be supportively close and available while approving and encouraging the developmental moves toward maturity and autonomous functioning.[2] Achieving an optimal balance between emotional availability to the developing child and letting go of the maturing child rests on a finely-tuned, parental empathy and ability to gauge the child's readiness for the next step in separation-individuation. This balancing brings to mind the medical dictum that the proper dose of any medication is enough and not too much.

Various observers have offered explanations for maternal difficulty in being appropriately available to the child. Mahler and

---

[2]The importance of autonomy throughout the life course and the role of its impairment in mental illness are compellingly set forth by Appel (2000) in *Who's in Charge: Autonomy and Mental Disorder.*

her research colleagues observed a lack of emotional availability in mothers who were unable to adjust to the progressive disengagement or increased demandingness of the child in the practicing subphase (Mahler et al. 1975, p. 81). They also attributed a pathogenic effect to a given mother's defensive tendency to *overly detach* herself from her child as the child becomes differentiated (ibid, p. 211). In analyzing children with separation anxiety, I have found that the opposite parental tendency of "failing to detach" can be due to a mother's own unresolved separation anxiety. The mother's separation anxiety is eased by holding onto her child rather than sanctioning individuation and with it separation. Other explanations for undesirable maternal influence have been adduced.

- If the mother steps down to the child's level, empathy and availability suffer and she cannot distinguish her needs from those of her child (Olden 1958).
- A mother who refuses her child the right to grow up is a mother who is dependent on the child for the satisfaction of her own needs (Buxbaum 1950).
- Failure of the mother–infant dyad to achieve emotional regulation impairs separation–individuation (Schore 1994).
- Lack of affective reciprocity between mother and infant is a factor in child neglect and abuse (Emde 1980).
- Unempathic parenting severely hinders the unfolding of the communicative process between child and parent (Blos 2000).
- The mother's being psychologically absent arrests and grossly distorts the child's development at its outset (Fraiberg 1982).

In the San Francisco research on parent–child interaction during the rapprochement subphase (Settlage 1989, 1992, 1993, 1994; Okimoto et al. 2001), the children reacted to the experience of libidinal loss with anger and anxiety. Clinical experience indicates that the child has a similar reaction to parental failure to approve and sanction increasing separation and independence. Because of the lack of direct observational research data about "failure to sanction," my discussion of pathogenesis is confined to reaction to loss.

Repression of Aggression

Whether overtly expressed or tacitly represented in hostile aggressive fantasies, aggression toward the parent is felt by the child to jeopardize the relationship already attenuated by loss. Repression of aggression can serve normal development or the formation of psychopathology at both the preoedipal and oedipal levels of development. Preoedipally, repression of aggression is evoked in the service of maintaining the needed nurturant and developmental relationship with the parent. My theory is that repression of an excessive amount of hostile aggression is the key pathogen in the impairment of preoedipal development and the formation of preoedipal psychopathology. My understanding of the developmental and psychopathological consequences of repression of aggression is conveyed in the following points.

1. Repression of hostile aggression means that aggressive feelings gain limited or no direct expression in the developmental interaction in later stages of development. Aggressive feelings are not confronted, labeled, mutually managed, and brought under modulated ego regulation by the child. Instead, they remain unchanged in the unconscious mind and are subjectively felt to be a potentially dangerous, internal liability. When stimulated by loss or threat of loss in a current important relationship, the repressed aggression threatens to breach the defense of repression and erupt in an uncontrolled aggressive act. Other defenses are then evoked to reinforce repression.

2. The felt or imagined destructive potential of repressed angry feelings and hostile destructive fantasies create anxiety about injuring or destroying the love object. The healthy assertive aggression required to achieve success in life is contaminated by the hostile aggression. Being assertive is subjectively felt to risk the release of the hostile aggression which could ride on the coattails of assertion. The consequent inhibition of assertive aggression interferes with the ability to function effectively. These dynamics unconsciously link achievement and success with destruction of the love object. The unconscious sense of one's destructive potential also engenders an unconscious fear of retaliation.

3. The combination of hostile destructive fantasies and the imagined power of omnipotence fantasies is felt to be extremely dangerous. Omnipotence fantasies are infantile defenses against feelings of helplessness and vulnerability. These combined fantasies create a strong expectation and fear of retaliation in kind. The unconsciously conceived punishment for destroying a love object is to be killed.

4. The unconscious fear of ones destructive potential toward others and the fear of retaliation can evoke the defense of "turning against the self." Although unconsciously serving to avoid greater harm at the hands of others, this defense ironically employs self-destructive behavior. The self-destruction can range from the sabotage of successful functioning in work and relationships, to self-destructive fantasies, sometimes including suicidal fantasies, to self-destructive acts such as neglect of one's health or the abuse use of drugs.

5. Repression of pathological, hostile aggression interferes with the structuring of object and self constancy, those preoedipal structures that serve respectively the regulation of relationships and the regulation of the sense of self. Adequate structuring involves the internalization of a predominance of loving experience over angry aggressive experience. Repressed, internally harbored, patho-

logical aggression prevents the desired predominance of loving experience. The consequent lack of regulatory structure causes arrest of the separation-individuation process.

6. Impairment of the development of object and self constancy and the resulting arrest of the separation-individuation process perpetuate excessive dependency. The dependency keeps the individual psychologically in the position of a child. Failure to grow up means that the adolescent child feels unprepared to move into adulthood. Assuming full adult responsibility for oneself yields to persistence of the childhood need to be loved and taken care of. In addition, the defense of not growing up and remaining a child psychologically nullifies the greater destructive capability associated with becoming an adult.

7. Not crossing the threshold into adulthood defers and denies the reality of eventual personal death at the end of adulthood. My clinical experience suggests that the inadequate structuring of object and self constancy is an important factor in the fear of facing one's eventual mortality. Impairment of these structures deprives the individual of the inner sense of being loved and cared about that underlies emotional equanimity and being at peace with oneself. When present, this inner sense makes it easier to accept the reality of one's own death.

Developmental Arrest

The concept of developmental arrest deserves elaboration. As was noted, arrest of the separation-individuation process perpetuates psychological dependency at the level of early childhood. The dependency embodies the child's need to be loved. Persistence of the need to be loved combined with the thrust to complete development cause the phenomenon of "keeping the door open to the past" (Settlage 1990, p. 39). This phenomenon metaphorically expresses the hope that the mother will change and lovingly meet the individual's needs neglected during childhood. In his analysis of adults, Akhtar (1991) uncovered and labeled three defensive fantasies spawned by dependency and the hope for parental change.

- *Tethering* keeps the individual tied to the parent.
- *Some day* expresses the hope that the parent will change.
- *Long embrace* imparts the wanted love.

The fantasy that the mother will change defends against acceptance of the injurious view of one's self as not being worthy of love and not being cared about and valued. This is why the fantasy persists even into adulthood. Tenaciously holding onto this fantasy precludes acceptance of the defacto loss of the developmentally needed love and the loss of the wished-for mother. Acceptance of these losses is a precondition for developmental relinquishment of the "mother-who-might-have-been." In childhood and adulthood, persistence of the wish for the *mother-who-might-have-been* tends to block growth-promoting interaction with developmental objects other than the parent (Settlage, Curtis, et al. 1988; Settlage 1992, 1994, 1996). Inevitably, though, the inadequately met need for love, the yearning for love, and the urge to complete development are expressed in a hopeful, positive transference to new, potential developmental objects such as a teacher, mentor, or one's psychoanalyst.

Mahler emphasized the importance in normal preoedipal development of the defense of splitting being superceded by the defense of repression (Mahler et al. 1975, p. 211). Repression of normal amounts of hostile aggression diminishes the impairing influence of conscious aggression in relationships. As described in point 5 under *Repression of Aggression*, repression of pathological amounts of hostile aggression interferes with the sound structuring of object and self constancy. Splitting is derived from the failure to sufficiently integrate bad experience with good experience in the development of these structures. The consequence is the formation of fragile, unstable, constancy structures that lend themselves to the defense of splitting.

Evoked by feelings of loss or betrayal in an important current relationship, splitting serves to minimize the engendered injury to the sense of self. Splitting changes the previously well-regarded or ambivalently regarded love object into an all-bad object (Settlage 1989, p. 386). At the same time, it staves off the defense of turning the aroused aggression against the self. Instead, it creates a compensatory representation of an all good self. Because the all-bad representation of the love object is not compatible with a good sense of self, the object is ejected from the internal world. This psychological reexternalization temporarily wipes out the good as well as the bad representations of experience with the object. The binding of bad by good experience cannot be achieved. The desired process of structural integration is disrupted and kept in a state of flux. Repression of pathological aggression and the defense of splitting interfere not only with the structuring of object and self constancy but with the normal developmental progression from splitting to repression.

RELINQUISHMENT AND MOURNING

The experience of loss in the relationship with the mother is built into normal development. With each step in the developmental progression there is a parallel relinquishment of involvement with the mother. Mahler (1961, 1966) identified the child's affective expressions of sadness and grief during development as the first signs of a letting go of the mother in external reality. The short-lived affective responses of sadness and grief in the child are the precursors of the longer-term responses of grief and mourning in the adult.

The developmental letting go of the mother is correlated with the establishment of an intrapsychic image of the mother.

This begins in the latter half of the first year during the practicing subphase (Mahler et al. 1975). Its establishment is inferred to be taking place, for example, during the child's state of "low-keyedness" in response to the temporary absence of the mother in Mahler's research situation. The inference is that the child in this subdued emotional state is imaging both the mother and experiences with the mother. The defensive objective of the imaging is to contain the separation anxiety. The imaging also serves internalization and representation of the mother in the child's internal world. The process of psychic representation associated with relinquishment in development is very similar to the process of psychic representation associated with mourning. They differ in that the object is still alive and present during relinquishment and is dead and gone during mourning. Developmental relinquishment would appear to be the prototype for mourning. If, however, separation-individuation is arrested and the mother is not relinquished, the prototype for mourning is not developed. This impairs the capacity for mourning.

Arrest of the separation-individuation process can impair and prolong the mourning process. Because the unresolved childhood dependency is displaced to the current love object, loss of the current object exposes the unrecognized dependency and reawakens the childhood feelings of insecurity, helplessness, and unworthiness. The resulting anxiety and feelings of despair are at first defended by denial of the loss and deferral of its acceptance. The mourning process cannot be effectively engaged until the loss of the object is accepted. These difficulties are exemplified by the case of Kate.

ILLUSTRATIVE CASE MATERIAL

The main purpose of the case material is to demonstrate that repressed aggression is the *key pathogen* in preoedipal pathology.

The Case of Ira

Ira was referred for treatment at age 3½ because of severe separation anxiety present since age 2. Although his anxiety could occur with any separation from his parents, it was particularly intense at night when his parents went out and left him with a sitter. Ira's early childhood loss experiences included:

- His mother's becoming pregnant with a second child when Ira was 22 months old and the resulting shift of some of her libidinal investment away from Ira to the future baby;
- The decreased libidinal availability of his mother due to her absorption with the need to find and set up a new home for the soon-to-be enlarged family;
- His mother's consequent, frequent absences.
- Loss of relationship with his father due to father's preoccupation with establishing his business and father's frequent absences on business trips.

A more subtle loss was uncovered during one of my meetings with Ira's mother. Persistence of the night-time separation anxiety and its occurrence even when Ira's parents were at home led to a bedtime ritual in which one of the parents, usually his mother, would lie beside Ira on his bed while he was falling asleep. Ira's mother revealed that waiting for him to fall asleep made her restless. As soon as she thought he was asleep, she would get up to leave him. No matter how quietly she left his side, he would become fully awake and protest her leaving. Exploring the reason for her restlessness led me to conclude that the sleep-time situation with Ira activated his mother's unresolved separation anxiety. Ira's falling asleep was disrupting her libidinal tie to him and her defense was to leave him emotionally, and physically, before he left her by falling asleep. Ira experienced her emotional withdrawal as a libidinal loss even though she was lying beside him.

Some years before my work with Ira, I learned about unfrequently leaving him for a time emotionally and physically when he was a little boy. As a little boy, though, he could not express his angry feelings because he so much needed and depended upon his parents.

I hoped the exchange Ira and I had in these few sessions would help resolve the pathology underlying his separation anxiety and facilitate the work with his new therapist.

The Case of Ilana

Ilana is an attractive, articulate, highly intelligent, capable lawyer. She was referred to me at age 28 by a Southern California analyst who treated her for two years before she moved to San Francisco. She is the oldest of three sisters. Her presenting problem was severe, life-long separation anxiety. Her chief complaints were her fear of flying and her failure to pass the bar examinations in eight tries. During the course of the analysis, the fear of flying subsided and she now can fly without experiencing her former panicky anxiety. Six months into the analysis, she passed the bar examinations. But her pattern of self-sabotage continued. She did not aggressively and effectively build her law practice. She greatly procrastinated over doing her professional work, and she charged too low a fee for her services. Because of her failure patterns, which included being overweight and not dieting and exercising, her boyfriend whom she later married refused marriage for several years.

Ilana's history of loss included experience with her very self-involved mother who was inconsistently available during Ilana's early childhood years and similar experience with her father. Her father was heavily engaged in his business and he dispensed constant criticism and very little love and empathy to his family. During Ilana's oedipal and latency years she was unable to stay overnight at schoolmates' homes. She walked to and from the nearby grade school. Walking home after school, Ilana never knew whether mother would be at home. If her mother's car was not

conscious sensitivity to libidinal loss during the analysis of a 10-year-old boy. George was the oldest of four siblings. In an abrupt shift away from the theme of prior treatment sessions, he invented a game called "hide the baby." In this game, one of us would hide a tiny plastic baby doll in the play room or in the adjacent room where I saw adults and the other would find it. After a couple of weeks of playing this game and not being able to fathom the reason for it, I had one of my periodic meetings with George's mother. She informed me that just that morning she found out she was again pregnant. The reason for George's game became evident. He unconsciously knew that his mother was pregnant before she consciously let herself know she was pregnant. Having lived through three of his mother's pregnancies, George had become well attuned to the shift of his mother's libidinal investment away from the external world and him to the fetal child in her womb.

Ira was 12 years old when I moved to Arkansas. In school, he was a straight-A student and he excelled at sports. The separation anxiety had greatly eased. He could, for example, sleep in his own room when traveling with his parents. Because his separation anxiety was not fully alleviated, I referred him for further treatment.

After I left California, I talked with Ira several times by telephone. Our talks were friendly but they did not take on the character of treatment sessions. I subsequently met with him in the living room of my hotel suite during several of my return visits to California. Prior to the first meeting, I learned from his mother about his experience in the realm of loss during the several months following my departure. He became absorbed with the news of a mass suicide by members of a cult and the news of the deaths of climbers on Mt. Everest. He had thoughts about death and reincarnation. He also had a dream in which he was going to commit suicide. In the dream, he was taking his leave, in his words, "quickly and peacefully" blowing himself up with gasoline.

The first return visit began as a warm reunion. Because I had experienced expressions of anger about my leaving from other patients, I soon asked him whether he was angry at me for going away. He said, "No." During the remainder of the time, though, he assiduously played and expressed angry aggression in "who is going to kill whom" games on the hotel television set. I felt that his exclusive absorption with the games reversed our positions at the time of my leaving. He now was abandoning me.

In the first of two sessions with Ira on my next visit, I again asked him if he was angry at me for leaving him. He replied, "Of course not." He picked up the pen and the small pad beside the telephone and began to make sketches. Shortly, he showed me that he was drawing a picture of a clown. The clown had a big bulbous nose, huge ears, and a bandage on his forehead. In several sketches, with increasing vigor Ira made the clown increasingly ugly. When he did not respond to my inquiries about his drawing the clown, I told him that I thought the clown might be me. I said the huge nose reminded me of his frequent complaint during therapy that I was too nosy, always prying into his personal business. I also said that the huge ears reminded me of his resentment about my hearing things about him from his mother. He silently continued to sketch.

A few minutes later, I asked about the bandage on the clown's head, noting that the bandage indicated something was wrong with the clown's head. He remained silent. I offered the thought that the damaged head might represent my head. After all, something must be mentally wrong with a guy who can abandon people who are counting on him. He again was silent and continued to sketch.

When two indecipherable drawings turned out to be parts of a machine gun, I said I found it interesting that he drew a weapon. Perhaps he *was* angry at me even though he said he was not. His reaction was to scribble away the clown, redraw him, and again scribble him away. In subsequent sketches, Ira's feelings about my leaving him were clearly expressed. On a drawing of an airplane in the sky, he wrote in hillbilly vernacular, "I'm going to Arkansas, yo-all." People are tumbling out of the plane as it soars

on its way. In the next drawing, the plane explodes and the remaining passengers, except one, fall to their death. The exception turns out to be the pilot who has insured his own safety by having a parachute. As the pilot floats to the ground, he calls the people falling to their deaths, "Scums!" In the final drawing of the series, Ira writes "Hi S." He always referred to me as Doctor S. Note that he took away my status as a doctor. He wrote two comments pointed at me: "Time to milk the cows" and "All butter and churn." He knew I was living on a farm.

In the second session, Ira complained that the phone pad was too small and availed himself of my larger letter-size pad. I saw his rejection of the phone pad as an unconscious expression of how he felt about talking to me by long-distance telephone. With an angry tone, Ira more forcefully pursued the theme of the preceding session. Several times the point of the pen tore into the paper. He sketched a plane that explodes and burns. He wrote, "All is disaster, but this guy has a parachute!"

Ira's communications by sketch are easily decoded. The pilot of Ira's therapy saves himself in a harshly uncaring way and doesn't provide his passenger patient with a lifesaving parachute. The final drawing unequivocally depicted a machine gun, now assemble and finely detailed. Below it, Ira sketched the same ugly clown b now with one arm raised as if to wave goodbye. Perhaps the of waving goodbye was an indication that Ira was in the pr of mastering the traumatic loss. He had moved from the or position of passively suffering loss to the position of a dealing with it, but his anger was still there. He again s away the clown.

When I persisted in giving Ira the opening, he f able to express his hostile aggressive feelings toward m that the lifting of the repression of his patholog required Ira's becoming disabused of his unconscio destructiveness. I therefore told him that I was express his anger toward me for leaving him. I a had the same angry feelings toward his parents in

in the driveway, Ilana would circle the block she lived on until mother arrived. When away at college, Ilana immediately found and symbiotically attached herself to a boyfriend. They shared an apartment and she did everything possible to avoid being separated from him. For example, she enrolled in the classes he was taking even if they were of no interest to her. She was demonstrating unresolved dependency and the need for interaction with an external object in the regulation of her emotions. Her need to repress angry feelings kept them from being expressed in relationships. Instead of confronting and engaging in dialogue about interpersonal issues, she skillfully employed artful and arcane manipulative strategies.

At the time of the first consultative visit, I told Ilana that two years from then I would be retiring and moving away. That information did not deter her from entering treatment with me. She and I were not yet aware of the severity of her pathology. She thought that a couple of years would be enough time for successful treatment. With hindsight, I think that her entering treatment with me was motivated by the unconscious urge for mastery and the hope that this time separation would not be traumatic.

Our geographic separation took place after two and a half years of analysis. Even though we had agreed to continue treatment by telephone, Ilana was woefully upset and cried copiously during the final two weeks of therapy sessions. In the next to last session, she gave me the gift of an attractive, hand-thrown, pottery bowl. Running her finger around the bulging curve of the bowl, she said, "Its surface is never ending." She was aware that her gift expressed the wish that our relationship would never end. My response to her giving me this gift and her wish that our relationship would never end had two determinants. One was my now being aware of her impaired object and self constancy and the other was my understanding that these psychic structures can be strengthened through developmental interaction with the analyst. I therefore wanted to mitigate the impact of my leaving on her underdeveloped structure and maintain my suitability as a devel-

opmental object. In the last session, I gave her a pottery bud vase
from my office desk. She later told me that she kept it on her office
desk.

When we resumed work by telephone a month later Ilana
said, "I thought you would always be here." She reported experiencing both loss and anger in the wake of my departure. She
would get up in the middle of the night and drive around the
streets near my California office. This behavior was reminiscent
of her walking around the block after school when her mother
was not at home. While driving, the words of a song entered her
mind: "I miss you like the desert misses the rain." Another song
came to mind. In this song, a woman is singing that she wants
to kill the woman who is the center of attention. Ilana exclaimed,
"Separation is the kiss of death!" In a later phone session, I pointed
out that my leaving her was for my benefit and at her expense.
I said that my behavior was like the similarly self-serving behavior
of her mother. Ilana cried. I felt that acknowledgement of my
leaving her as being self-serving would help neutralize the belief
commonly held by children that they are abandoned because of
their unworthiness as it is reified by conscious or unconscious
anger toward the parent, now me in the transference.

The phone sessions took place at 7:00 A.M. California time.
After some months of work, Ilana revealed that she usually talked
to me while still in bed. Ilana's first reenactment of the postulated
libidinal loss while falling asleep as an infant followed a "big fight"
with her mother. Because she felt that her mother was being very
unempathic, Ilana screamed at her, "You are wrong! You are self-
ish!" I noted that she had allowed herself to express her long-
repressed rage and that her mother did not drop dead. Ilana
stopped talking. After a minute or so she began to breathe slowly
and deeply. She asked, "Do you hear how heavily I am breathing?
It's amazing!" She said she was falling asleep. Her silence and deep
breathing continued. After a short time, she said that it now was
close to the time her husband leaves for work. She earlier told me
that she moves to his side of the bed when he gets up in the

morning. The heat from his body warms his side of the bed and lying in his warmth makes her feel that he is still there and they are not separated. After more heavy breathing, she said she was almost asleep. Suspecting that Ilana was reenacting with me the experience of libidinal loss while falling asleep as an infant, and that her mother's defensive emotional withdrawal precluded internalization of mother as available and caring during the sleep-time separation, I said that maybe she wanted to take me with her as she fell asleep.

In the next session, I asked Ilana what she thought about falling asleep. She replied, "Separation." She said she has always had trouble falling asleep. She remembered staying asleep in the morning and being late for school. She told me that her mother had always stayed in bed in the morning and did not prepare breakfast for her or see her off to school. Ilana was alone and on her own. Not so parenthetically, Ilana told me during the treatment that her mother's mother had a terrible, life-long separation anxiety. Unresolved separation anxiety can be passed on from generation to generation. I offered Ilana two reasons for her staying asleep and not wanting to go to school. She did not want to separate from her mother and did not want to return home from school and find that mother was not there.

Some months later, the infantile sleep transference appeared in another session. Ilana said she was lying in bed in a fetal position. It felt like being in a cocoon. The word *cocoon* reminded me that the word *develop* means to unfold and no longer be enveloped, like a chick emerging through the eggshell. I thought that her imagery could be an unconscious expression of her need and wish to resume development or perhaps to begin her life anew. Ilana asked me if I was tired and wanted to take a nap. She had an image of me in a lounge chair with my head back and my eyes closed, "as though you are lying beside me like a parent lying next to a child at the child's bedtime." Being aware of the sexual implication of her fantasy, she qualified the image and feelings as expressing the closeness of a parent and a young child and not being erotically charged. I, too, felt that she was expressing the basic, generic love of the preoedipal, mother–infant relationship which is to be distinguished from the genital, sexual love of the oedipal and later stages of development (Settlage 1996, p. 556).

In the next session she said, "I'm still waking up. Get me a pacifier." She talked about how nice it was to fall asleep with me there on the phone at the other end of the line. I said that maybe the phone connection means that we are not separated. She said that being connected by the telephone line is like being connected by an infinitely elastic umbilical cord.

Although the presented evidence of preverbal experience is inferred, it does seem to support the hypothesis that Ilana was reenacting infantile sleep experience with her mother. She was undoing with me the loss of relationship caused by her mother's emotional withdrawal before Ilana was fully asleep. She then could restructure her object constancy by internalizing the experience of my being emotionally available.

Clinical material from the analysis of Ilana also pertains to repressed aggression. She reported a "weird" dream that occurred after her husband had "harassed" her about her obesity. In the dream, daylight was turning into darkness. The sky became filled with a huge black cloud of dirt that was exuding something "yucky." She "summoned" her husband from the house to see this ominous phenomenon. He looked at the black cloud and fell to the ground in a dead faint, smothered by the dirt in the air. Ilana dragged him into the house and he recovered consciousness.

Mentioning that her husband is very unhappy about her body, Ilana wondered whether the black cloud represented her body: "Is my body exuding something destructive?" I said that the destructive cloud she put in her dream did nearly kill her husband. She connected the cloud with her anger at her husband for chastising her. She remembered that she thought about her mother after awakening from the dream. Her mother has been on portable oxygen because of damage to her lungs from years of smoking. I said the dream seemed to verify the interpretation that she

unconsciously feared that release of her repressed aggression wou[ ]
destroy her loved ones, both her husband and her mother. I als[ ]
pointed out that the dream was a sign of progress. I told her that
allowing herself to express her rageful feelings in a dream meant
that she had become less fearful of her destructive potential.

Ilana appears to be "turning the corner." She is doing well
in her law practice. Her manipulative mode is fading and she now
is able to be more open and direct in dealing with interpersonal
matters. She resolutely has begun to diet and exercise.

The Case of Kate

Kate is now a 65-year-old woman whom I saw in analysis from
age 53 to age 61. She is the mother of three grown children. The
clinical material pertinent to this paper comes from the analytic
work resumed by telephone when she was 63. I will describe the
presenting picture at the time of the original analysis but will not
discuss the analysis itself.

At age 53, Kate felt that time was running out. She feared
that she would not fulfill her ambition of making a major contribution to humankind. Although very creative and effective in
carrying out her family-, social-, and community-service activities,
she also experienced undue stress and anxiety. Kate also was
convinced that aging was robbing her of the attractiveness she saw
as her prime asset in getting people to like and work with her.
Yet, she still is a very attractive woman whose features, personality,
and flair for dressing in a creative, elegant way garner admiring
attention.

The patient's early childhood was marked by a self-centered
mother who established a close alliance with Kate's older sister that
excluded Kate. This gave Kate an unremitting, lifelong fear of
being "left out" of relationships. She felt that her mother did not
care for her and was only minimally emotionally available. She had
a good relationship with her father who was her hero in her

ntasy life. But he left the family and disappeared from Kate's life when she was a young teenager.

During her childhood, Kate felt that she had to make it on her own. In keeping with Freud's concept of the formation and function of the ego–ideal as response to early libidinal loss (Freud 1914, Jacobson 1964, Settlage 1973, p. 80), her ambition was to prove her worth and gain love and approval through outstanding achievements. She indeed had many outstanding successes and was loved and valued. When not in the limelight, though, she felt unwanted and worthless.

Kate contacted me a month after the death of her husband. She recounted the automobile accident. She and her husband were crossing the Sierra Mountains during a snowstorm. She was driving. They encountered black, glare ice on a sharp curve in the road. The car slid uncontrollably off of the road and crashed down the mountainside. Her husband was ejected and killed instantly. She suffered multiple fractures of her pelvis and legs. We talked by phone once a week for several months. My purpose was to help her accept her loss and begin the mourning process. Her emotions were very intense and expressed an admixture of guilt, grief, despair, and anxiety. She had episodes of panic about being "all alone." She foresaw only a completely dismal life. Kate had great difficulty accepting her loss and her mourning process was characterized by repeated cycles of progress followed by reversion to depressive feelings and despair. We decided to resume treatment.

The Therapeutic Dialogue

The following material is excerpted from selected sessions held during the first 15 months of the resumed analysis. It portrays the nature of the therapeutic dialogue. During the first month of the treatment, Kate's verbalizations were interspersed with crying. She made frequent appeals for help crying out, "Oh God! Help me!"

She felt like a little girl who had no one to turn to. "My husband is gone and I can't live without him." She thought of going to a mental hospital and of suicide. Throughout the treatment, though, she manifested great courage and staying power in facing and dealing with her huge loss and its damaging effects.

She talked about the accident. "I'm angry about my husband's leaving me. I didn't do it. It was an accident. I think he was ready to go." I wondered whether her anger at him made her feel she did kill him. She responded, "No. Yes. I don't know." She cried out, "I am hopeless. I have no future!" I noted that feeling hopeless could be a way of curbing her anger and guilt because she survived her husband and unconsciously blamed herself for his death. I said she could not let herself entertain the idea of having a good, successful life alone and on her own. Her reply was, "Whenever I get good at something, as I did in my textile weaving, I stop doing it." This is reminiscent of Ilana's more overt self-sabotage.

The content of the treatment to this point suggested that Kate's loss of her husband had exposed a previously veiled, unrecognized dependency on him. During the original analysis, I had not perceived the extent of dependency on her husband.

Kate continued to feel that her plight was devastating. She said that she thought about ways to kill herself. The intensity of her feelings led me to think that her reaction to the loss of her husband was compounded by the unmourned loss of the mother she yearned for as a child and still yearned for as an adult, and by the inadequately mourned loss of her father when she was a teenager. I shared this thought with Kate.

She talked about how terrible the accident was and asked, "How come I didn't have your Arkansas phone number?" Since I had given her my number, I wondered whether she might have mislaid it. She said, "No, but maybe I didn't carefully keep it because I didn't need it." I suggested the alternative explanation that she had unconsciously experienced my moving away as a repeat of the abandonment by her mother and father, and that in the analysis she was giving vent to her anger toward me and also to her long-repressed, resentful feelings toward her parents. She responded, "Thanks for putting up with me."

Kate said she felt her life was unstructured. "I have always had to keep busy—to screen out my demons." I observed that her husband provided structure and that his presence bolstered her ego in warding off her demons. She volunteered that keeping busy probably was a way of escaping her feelings. Abruptly, she had to go to the bathroom. Upon her return, she said that going to the bathroom in the middle of talking to me was amazing. In an embarrassed manner, she reported that she had an urgent bowel movement. I felt that Kate had momentarily regressed psychologically to the anal stage of psychosexual development and the parallel rapprochement subphase of separation–individuation. In the figurative position of a child in the second year of life she expressed her repressed aggression somatically in anal terms. I told her that the bowel movement no doubt was a non-verbal expression of her repressed rage. I added that she distanced herself from her rage by transforming it into demons. She said, "I'm so frightened. What if I didn't have you? I'd kill myself." It was clear that her unresolved dependency was being expressed in the transference to me.

During an in-person session in California, Kate told me that her husband was annoyingly critical of her on the morning of the accident. When they were on highway he fell asleep. She was angry at him for not being alertly with her when she was driving under such hazardous road conditions. In my terms, he libidinally abandoned her. She reported a dreAmerican In the dream, her 2-year-old granddaughter fell into a swimming pool and sank to the bottom. The little girl's father is flustered and hesitates before jumping in to rescue her. Kate felt that she was represented by her granddaughter who was in danger of drowning and not being rescued. At the end of the session she said, "I'm upset that you are leaving to return to Arkansas." After a teary-eyed pause, she said, "As a child, I thought I had to please people or they would leave me. I felt that not having someone meant to die." I said that she was experiencing my leaving her as the same kind of abandonment she had experienced in childhood. After a bit of reflection, I observed that remaining dependent and staying forever a child would be a way to avoid dying.

Kate reported another dreAmerican Someone was following her. That person was carrying body parts. Kate came to a precipitous overlook and "contemplated" jumping off—but did not think she would do so. She connected the "body parts" with her dead husband. "What if he was dismembered?" Mentioning that she had survived the accident, she said, "It didn't decapitate me." I called her attention to her use of the word *decapitate*. She uncomfortably revealed that she had the thought that her husband might have been decapitated when she was lying at the bottom of the mountain-side immediately after the accident. I said that her now thinking about decapitation in relation to herself was prompted by her guilt about the accident having occurred with her at the wheel. Her decapitation would have ended her life, too. She then would have been spared her loss and all of the her pain and misery. She said, "I see that."

The Process of Change

The following material is from the sixteenth through the twenty-seventh months of treatment. It conveys the nature of the mourning process and therapeutic process, and the progression of favorable change in Kate's emotional equilibrium and functioning. The citations were scattered over the eleven-month period. I have pulled them together for the sake of coherence.

Kate observed that, "Life is a wheel of grief. I need to draw on my memories but I can't embrace them until I accept that my loss is forever." Even though Kate in her reading about mourning had seen a diagram of a "wheel of grief," it seems safe to say that her use of the term was unconsciously connected to the fact of her being at the steering wheel of the car at the time of the tragic accident.[3] In saying, "Life is a wheel of grief," Kate captured the cyclic nature of her mourning process. For many months, every advance she made to a state of feeling good and beginning to enjoy life was quickly followed by a state of grief, despair, and feeling that she could not live this way. The cycles were symptomatic of her resistance to accepting the loss of her husband and the loss of her dependency. To accept these losses meant that she would have to face and resolve her repressed hostile aggression and her childhood feelings of insecurity and helplessness. She then would need to learn how to take care of herself. Because her dependency kept her psychologically in some ways in the position of a child, she was frightened and daunted by these prospects even though she in fact had the capability to cope with life on her own.

Recognizing her repetitive pattern of doing well and then being set back, Kate said, "Giving up is like dying, yet not really dying. I feel I have to die, at least a little. My life is over." I commented that only her former life is over and said that she is mourning the loss of her former life as well as the loss of her husband. She said, "The obligation to live is killing me. It is a heavy mantle. But I don't like the idea of dying. I fear death. Resistance to mortality kills us all." My response was to say that not forging ahead with her new life would be a kind of suicide.[4]

Despite its repetitious cycles, Kate's mourning process progressed and began to free her from the entangling ties to her lost husband. As she came to terms with her loss, there were signs of hope. She was still discouraged but not mainly because her husband was gone. Now it was because she was afraid of taking responsibility for her life. "If I don't stay sad and continue to have

---

[3] I am indebted to M. Robert Gardner, M.D. for this insightful observation.

[4] I owe this thought to Spencer H. Bloch, M.D., a colleague with whom I discussed this case.

a problem, I can't expect to be rescued. So I stay sad and cling to my misery. But I don't want the misery to end. Ending my misery would be like a rejection, like being left out." She also had the thought that not being in the limelight was like dying a little. As was noted in the earlier reference to the ego-ideal, beginning in her childhood years and to the present Kate has been preoccupied with gaining love and approval. This has been her *modus vivendi*. She said she now realized that she had a choice. "I can continue to gather evidence that I am unloved and unwanted or I can 'kick that,' accept that my husband really is gone, and start loving myself."

Kate talked to a friend about not getting help from outside. "I need to have the courage to rescue myself. That's a major shift for me." After what I took to be a reflective pause she said, "The idea of rescuing myself made me realize that talking to you about suicide is the ultimate appeal. It is an urgent appeal for you to rescue me." I had earlier shared the concept of the appeal cycle with Kate. I wanted her to understand that distress and anger are natural reactions to the loss of relationship with the parent and that the child's appeal to the parent is normal.

Kate drew on her experience as a weaver and said, "Making a new life is like making a weaving. Both are created thread by thread." Kate's metaphor reminded me of a similar metaphor in a dream of another patient who had lost her husband (Settlage 1996). In that patient's dream, she had lost a knitting needle and was trying to find a match for the one she still had. I said to this patient that it is not possible to knit with only one needle, and that being alone and not having her husband made it very difficult for her to refabricate her life.

Kate expressed the thought that she was turning the tables on her husband. He had abandoned her and left her a little girl at the bottom of the mountainside. Mourning and letting go of him was abandoning him. She recently had noticed that she was using memories of her husband's caring for her to soothe and comfort herself. "I am doing it my way and for myself." I said that the internalization of the experience of being soothed normally takes place in infancy and is a first step toward independence and autonomy of function. She now was taking a developmental step that her deficient emotional experience with her mother did not enable when she was a child.

Kate noted another change. She had directly asked her son and daughter-in-law for help. "My asking just popped out. In the past, I would not directly ask for help because I feared not receiving it." I said that her not asking for help and not risking rejection also avoided the hurt that would stir up her repressed anger.

She said that she was emerging from "the great pool of abandonment." I saw the word *pool* to be an unconscious reference to the dream in which Kate's granddaughter was in danger of drowning. Kate next said, "But I can cry at the drop of a hat over the life I am to lead. If my husband were alive, or I had a replacement for him, all would be fine." I said that having her husband or a substitute for him would maintain her dependent adaptation but then her development would remain incomplete. She replied, "I do understand what you have been telling me. My anger has been somewhat mollified. I trust myself and can count on myself. I am a good person. The universe is aligning for me to make it."

I see the favorable changes in Kate's emotional state and attitude as being due to her coming to grips with her repressed aggression and to the strengthening of her constancy structures. Earlier, I said that the unfulfilled need for love and completion of development is expressed in a positive transference to potential developmental objects other than the parents. Elsewhere I have expressed the view that the analyst is a developmental object as well a transference object (Settlage 1992, 1993, 1994, 1996). I think that Kate's interaction with me as a developmental object contributed to a favorable restructuring of her object and self constancy.

CLOSING COMMENTS

Preoedipal Experience

Both the child's need for love and the experience of libidinal loss are inherent in human development. Being loved, valued, and respected by the parents favors the overall development of the child who is so regarded. But no parent is capable of functioning ideally at all times. Inconsistency in libidinal availability is inevitable. Most parents do their devoted best in rearing their children. But aspects of the parent's emotional development and functioning commonly have been impaired by their own childhood experience. In addition, the child's experience of the parent is negatively distorted by the tendency of children to project their repressed aggression onto the parent. The parent's actions are then felt to be more malevolent than they actually are. Generally, the mild to moderate degrees of structural impairment and separation anxiety resulting from usual degrees of inconsistent availability do not significantly impair functioning. Also, if subsequent parental and other important relationships are basically good, these impairments can be reworked to a better outcome in subsequent stages of life-long development (Goodman 1977, pp. 56-60).

Freud's Theory of the Etiology of Neuroses

In his final summation of the basic tenets of psychoanalysis, Freud wrote about his lack of understanding of the role of the aggressive instinct in pathogenesis (Freud 1940, p. 185, Settlage 1994, p.28). His observations had shown that repression seemed to arise invariably from the component instincts of the sexual life. Yet psychoanalytic theory suggested that the demands of the aggressive instinct should cause the same kind of repressions and pathological consequences. Referring to this as a gap in theory that could not at that time be filled, he indicated that it remained to be decided whether the large part sexuality plays in the causation of neurosis is an exclusive one.

I think that the presented conceptualization of repressed aggression and the postulate that repressed aggression is the key pathogen in preoedipal pathology helps fill Freud's gap in theory. When Freud expressed his dissatisfaction, his focus was on neurosis and its etiology in unresolved oedipal conflict. I attribute Freud's difficulty in closing the gap in theory to two factors. Because of its largely preverbal and unrememberable nature, Freud in his self-analysis did not have the same access to his preoedipal experience as he had to his oedipal experience. Secondly, he did not have the benefit of today's knowledge of preoedipal development and psychopathology as it has been greatly expanded in recent decades by clinical explorations (e.g. Kohut 1971, Kernberg 1975) and by direct observational research on infant development as cited in this paper.

Psychoanalytic Technique

In his final summation, Freud (1940, pp. 172–182) discussed *The Technique of Psychoanalysis*. He underscored the extreme importance of transference and characterized it as being "*ambivalent:* it comprises positive (affectionate) as well as negative (hostile) attitudes toward the analyst, who as a rule is put in the place of one or the other of the patient's parents, his father or mother." After a cautionary observation about the possibility of an easy, false, "transference cure," Freud notes that the patient's placing the analyst in the "father (or mother)" position gives the analyst the power which the patient's superego exercises over the patient's ego. "The new super-ego, now has the opportunity for a sort of after-education of the neurotic; it can correct the mistakes for which the parents were responsible in educating him." Freud warns against the analyst's misusing this new influence and simply repeating a mistake of the parents in crushing the child's independence, thus only replacing the patient's earlier dependence by a new one. Freud then makes an intriguing statement: "The amount of influence which [the analyst] may legitimately use will be determined by the degree of *developmental inhibition* (my italics) present in the patient. Some neurotics have remained so infantile that in analysis too they can only be treated as children"

Exactly what Freud means by *after-education* and by *developmental inhibition* is not clear, and he gives no details about technique as it relates to these concepts or to his observation that infantile neurotics "can only be treated as children." In his comments about the superego and the neurotic patient, Freud is focused on development and pathogenesis at the oedipal level. But his description of some neurotics as remaining infantile would seem to indicate Freud's awareness of earlier developmental inhibition and preoedipal pathogenesis. The phrase *"in analysis too"* suggests that he is juxtaposing the psychoanalytic situation and the parenting situation. I cite this uncharacteristically unclear passage as further evidence that, for the reasons mentioned above, Freud had not fathomed the now known intricacies of preoedipal development and psychopathology beyond perceiving the role of the oral and anal stages of psychosexual development.

In my thinking, *after-education* and relief of *developmental inhibition* are effected through the patient's interaction with the analyst as a developmental object, using the analyst in accordance with the patient's developmental needs. This is not because the analyst acts like a parent and exercises parental authority or seeks to impose personal values on the patient but because the psychoanalytic position in relation to the patient makes the analyst a suitable developmental object (Settlage 1996, p. 556, Sandler, Kennedy, and Tyson 1980). *Developmental interaction* is enabled when the undoing of pathology in a given area of personality development opens up that area for resumption of development (Settlage 1992, p. 355). The patient's use of the analyst as a developmental object can be enhanced by adding a *developmental stance* to the usual psychoanalytic stance (Settlage 1992, pp. 356–360).

Since its inception in the mind of Freud, psychoanalysis has been subject to change in theory and technique first of all by Freud himself. Loewald's (1960) analogy between the parent–child relationship and the analyst–patient relationship and Stone's (1961) conceptualization of the analyst as the mother of separation, brought preoedipal as well as later developmental experience within the scope of therapeutic analysis. In addition to the resolution of intrapsychic conflict associated with oedipal pathogenesis, therapeutic analysis involves the confrontation, interpretation, undoing, and mastery of injurious, preoedipal experiences.

The treatment and resolution of preoedipal psychopathology rests centrally on the analysis of the repressed hostile aggression. The analysis of repressed aggression requires that it be exposed, experienced, and mastered. Because this process brings the subjectively felt, unconscious fear of its destructive potential into conscious awareness, the uncovering is met with strong unconscious resistance. The fear of the destructive potential of hostile aggression evokes the defensive attitude epitomized in the familiar adage, *let sleeping dogs lie.* But repressed aggression can be analyzed. It is necessary to persistently call the patient's attention to signs of inhibition of aggression and to inquire about the absence of aggression when its presence and expression would be expected. This needs to be done in keeping with the patient's tolerance for the threatening aggressive feelings and fantasies. The appropriate technique for such gradual exposure of repressed aggression is that of defense analysis (Settlage 1974, Gray 1994). The presented thoughts about treatment and resumption of development are most applicable in cases where the child–parent interaction, despite its lacks, has been sufficiently good that the individual continues to seek new developmental experience.

Margaret Mahler's decision to directly observe and study mother–infant interaction enabled her and her research colleagues to perceive the role of love and healthy, assertive aggression in the service of development alongside the pathogenic role of repressed aggression in response to libidinal loss. Separation-individuation theory stands alongside Freud's psychosexual theory as a major contribution to our understanding of child development. It also has provided and still provides a much needed basis for the application of the psychoanalytic method to preoedipal psychopathology.

REFERENCES

Ainsworth, M.D.S. and Wittig, B.A. (1969). Attachment theory and exploratory behavior of 1-year-olds in a strange situation. In *Determinants of Infant Behavior*, ed. B.M. Foss. London: Metheun, pp. 11–136.

Akhtar, S. (1991). Three fantasies related to unresolved separation-individuation: a less recognized aspect of severe character pathology. In *Beyond the Symbiotic Orbit: Advances in Separation-Individuation Theory*, ed. S. Akhtar and H. Parens, pp. 261–284. Hillsdale, NJ: The Analytic Press.

Appel, J.W. (2000). *Who's in Charge?: Autonomy and Mental Disorder.* Danbury, CT: Rutledge Books.

Blos, P., Jr. (2000). Psychic and somatic expressions of preverbal loss: analysis of a child adopted at thirteen months of age. In *Psychoanalysis in Childhood and Adolescence*, ed. K. Blitzing, P. Tyson, and Burgin. Basel: Karger press.

Buxbaum, E. (1950). Technique of terminating psychoanalysis. *International Journal of Psycho-Analysis*, 31:184–190.

Clyman, R.B. (1972). The procedural organization of emotions: a contribution from cognitive science to the psychoanalytic theory of therapeutic action. *Journal of the American Psychoanalytic Association*, 39 (S):349–389.

Decarie, T.J. (1965). *Intelligence and Affectivity in Early Childhood.* New York: International Universities Press.

Edelman, G.M. (1992). *Bright Air, Brilliant Fire: On the Matter of the Mind.* New York: Basic Books.

Emde, R.N. (1980). Toward a psychoanalytic theory of affect, II: Emerging models of emotional development in infancy. In *The Course of Life: Psychoanalytic Contributions Toward Understanding Personality Development, Vol. 1: Infancy and Early Childhood*, ed. S.I. Greenspan and G.H. Pollock. DHHS Publication No. (ADM) 80–786, pp. 85–112.

———. (1983). The representational self and its affective core. *The Psychoanalytic Study of the Child*, 38:165–192.

Escalona, S. (1968). *The Roots of Individuality: Normal Patterns of Development in Infancy.* Chicago: Aldine Publishing.

Fraiberg, S. (1982). Pathological defenses in infancy. *Psychoanalytic Quarterly,* 51:612–635.

Freud, A. (1946). *The Ego and the Mechanisms of Defence.* New York: International Universities Press.

Freud, S. (1914). On narcissism: an introduction. *Standard Edition.* 14:69–102. London: Hogarth Press.

————. (1920). Beyond the pleasure principle. *Standard Edition.* 18:7–64.

————. (1923). The ego and the id. *Standard Edition.* 19:12–66. London: Hogarth Press.

————. (1926). Inhibitions, symptoms, and anxiety. *Standard Edition.* 20:87–174. London: Hogarth Press.

————. (1930). Civilization and its discontents. *Standard Edition.* 21:64–145. London: Hogarth Press.

————. (1937). Analysis terminable and interminable. *Standard Edition.* 23:216–253. London: Hogarth Press.

Goodman, S., Editor (1977). *Psychoanalytic Research and Education: The Current Situation and Future Possibilities.* New York: International Universities Press.

Gray, P. (1994). *The Ego and the Analysis of Defense.* New York: Jason Aronson Inc.

Hall, (1999). The anatomy of fear. *New York Times Magazine,* February 28, Section 6., p. 42 et seq.

Jacobson, E. (1964). *The Self and the Object World.* New York: International Universities Press.

Kandel, E.R. (1983). From metapsychology to molecular biology: Explorations in the nature of anxiety. *American Journal of Psychiatry,* 156:505–524.

————. (1999). Biology and the future of psychoanalysis: a new intellectual framework for psychiatry revisited. *American Journal of Psychiatry,* 156:505–524.

Kernberg, O.F., (1975). *Borderline Conditions and Pathological Narcissism.* New York: Jason Aronson Inc.

————. (1980). *Internal World and External Reality: Object Relations Theory Applied.* New York: Jason Aronson Inc.

Kernberg, P. (1980). The origins of the reconstructed in psychoanalysis. In *Rapprochement,* ed. R.F. Lax, S. Bach, and J.A Burland. pp. 263–281. New York: Jason Aronson Inc.

Kohut, H. (1971). *The Analysis of the Self.* New York: International Universities Press.

Kramer, S. (1980). The technical significance and application of Mahler's separation-individuation theory. In *Psychoanalytic Explorations of Technique: Discourses on the Theory of Therapy,* ed. H. Blum. pp. 240–262. New York: International Universities Press.

Lear, J. (1990). *Love and Its Place in Nature: A Philosophical Interpretation of Freudian Psychoanalysis.* New Haven: Yale University Press.

Loewald, H.W. (1960). On the therapeutic action of psychoanalysis. *International Journal of Psycho-Analysis* 41:16–33.

Mahler, M.S. (1961). On sadness and grief in infancy and childhood: Loss and restitution of the symbiotic love object. *The Psychoanalytic Study of the Child,* 16:332–351.

———. (1966). Notes on the development of basic moods: the depressive affect. In *Psychoanalysis—a General Psychology: Essays in Honor of Heinz Hartmann,* ed. R.M. Loewenstein, L.M. Newman, M. Schur, and A.J. Solnit. pp. 152–168, New York: International Universities Press.

———. (1968). *On Human Symbiosis and the Vicissitudes of Individuation, Vol. 1: Infantile Psychosis.* New York: International Universities Press.

———. (1971). A study of the separation-individuation process and its possible application to borderline phenomena in the psychoanalytic situation. *The Psychoanalytic Study of the Child,* 26:403–424. New York: Quadrangle Books.

———. (1972). Rapprochement subphase of the separation-individuation process. *Psychoanalytic Quarterly,* 41:487–506.

Mahler, M.S. and McDevitt, J.B. (1968). Observations on adaptation and defense in statu nascendi: Developmental precursors in the first two years of life. *Psychoanalytic Quarterly,* 37:1–21.

Mahler, M.S., Pine, F., and Bergman, A. (1975). *The Psychological Birth of the Human Infant: Symbiosis and Individuation.* New York: Basic Books.

Novick, J. and Novick, K.K. (2000). Love in the therapeutic alliance. *Journal of the American Psychoanalytic Association,* 48:189–218.

Okimoto, J.T., Settlage, C.F., Freed, W., Klein, K., Dao, E., Campbell, J., Yoshiike, Y., Lui, B., and Mason, C. (2001). The appeal cycle phenomenon in three cultures: an exploratory cultural comparison of child development in the second year of life. *Journal of the American Psychoanalytic Association,* 49:187–215.

Olden, C. (1958). On adult empathy with children. *The Psychoanalytic Study of the Child,* 8:11–126. New York: International Universities Press.

Parens, H. and Saul, L.J. (1971). *Dependence in Man: A Psychoanalytic Study.* New York: International Universities Press.

Piaget, J. (1937). *The Construction of Reality in the Child.* New York: Basic Books, 1954.

Pine, F. (1986). The "symbiotic" phase in the light of current infancy research. *Bulletin of the Menninger Clinic,* 50:564–569.

Provence, S. and Lipton, R.C. (1962). *Infants in Institutions.* New York: International Universities Press.

Sander, L.W. (1962). Issues in early mother–child interaction. *Journal of the Academy of Child Psychiatry,* 1:141–166.

Sandler, J., Kennedy, H., Tyson, R.L. (1980). *The Technique of Child Analysis: Discussions with Anna Freud.* Cambridge, MA: Harvard University Press.

Schore, A.N. (1994). *Affect Regulation and the Origin of the Self: The Neurobiology of Emotional Development.* Hillsdale, N.J.: Lawrence Erlbaum.

Schur, M. (1966). *The Id and the Regulatory Principles of Mental Functioning.* New York: International Universities Press.

Settlage, C.F. (1973). Cultural values and the superego in late adolescence. *The Psychoanalytic Study of the Child,* 27:74–92.

———. (1974). The technique of defense analysis in the psychoanalysis of an early adolescent. In *The Analyst and the Adolescent at Work,* ed. M Harley. New York: Quadrangle Books, pp. 3–39.

———. (1989). The interplay of therapeutic and developmental process in the treatment of children: An application of contemporary object relations theory. *Psychoanalytic Inquiry,* 9:375–396.

———. (1990). Childhood to adulthood: structural change in development toward independence and autonomy. In *New Dimensions in Adult Development,* ed. R.A. Nemiroff and C.A. Colarusso. pp. 26–43, New York: Basic Books.

———. (1992). Psychoanalytic observations on adult development in life and in the therapeutic relationship. *Psychoanalytic . . . Contemporary Thought,* 15:349–374.

———. (1993). Therapeutic process and developmental process in the restructuring of object and self constancy. *Journal of the American Psychoanalytic Association,* 41:473–492.

———. (1994). On the contribution of separation-individuation theory to psychoanalysis: Development, psychopathology, and treatment. In *Mahler and Kohut: Perspectives on Development, Psychopathology, and Technique,* ed. S. Kramer and S. Akhtar. pp. 17–52. Northvale, NJ: Jason Aronson Inc.

———. (1996). Transcending old age: Creativity, development, and psychoanalysis in the life of a centenarian. *International Journal of Psycho-Analysis,* 77:549–564.

Settlage, C.F., Bemesderfer, S, Rosenthal, J., Afterman, J., and Spielman, P.M. (1991). The appeal cycle in early mother-child interaction: The nature and implications of a finding from developmental research. *Journal of the American Psychoanalytic Association,* 39:987–1014.

Settlage, C.F., Curtis, J., Lozoff, Marjorie, Lozoff, Milton, Silberschatz, G., and Simburg, E.J. (1988). Conceptualizing adult development. *Journal of the American Psychoanalytic Association,* 36:347–369.

Settlage, C.F., Rosenthal, J., Spielman, P.M., Gassner, S., Afterman, J., Bemesderfer, S., and Kolodny, S. (1990). An exploratory study of mother–child interaction during the second year of life. *Journal of the American Psychoanalytic Association,* 38:705–731.

Settlage, C.F., Silver, D.H., Afterman, J., Hart, K., and Nelson, K. (1993). Developmental process: Mother-child and father–child interaction during the second year of life.

In *Family, Self, and Society: Toward a New Agenda for Family Research*, ed. P.A. Cowan, D. Field, D. Hansen, E. Skolnick, and G.E. Swanson. pp. 363–384, Hillsdale, NJ: Lawrence Erlbaum.

Spitz, R.A. (1946). Anaclitic depression: An inquiry into the genesis of psychiatric conditions in early childhood. *The Psychoanalytic Study of the Child*, 2:313–342. New York: International Universities Press.

————. (1963). Ontogenesis: The proleptic function of emotion. In *The Expression of Emotions*, ed. P.H. Knapp. New York: International Universities Press.

————. (1964). The derailment of dialogue: Stimulus overload, action cycles, and the completion of gradient. 12:752–775.

————. (1965). *The First Year of Life: A Psychoanalytic Study of Normal and Deviant Development of Object Relations*. New York: International Universities Press.

Stern, D.N. (1985). *The Interpersonal World of the Infant*. New York: Basic Books.

Stone, L. (1961). *The Psychoanalytic Situation: An Examination of Its Development and Essential Nature*. New York: International Universities Press.

Trevarthen, C. (1979). Communication and cooperation in early infancy: A description of primary intersubjectivity. In *Before Speech: The Beginning of Interpersonal Communication*, ed. M.M. Bullowa. New York: Cambridge University Press.

5

FROM MENTAL PAIN THROUGH MANIC DEFENSE TO MOURNING

Discussion of Settlage's Chapter, "Defenses Evoked by Early Childhood Loss: Their Impact on Life-Span Development"

Salman Akhtar, M.D.

In seeking the origins of hysterical conversion symptoms, Freud (1895a, 1896) discovered the subterranean continuity of the effects of childhood trauma into adulthood. Later, he added that fantasized, and not actual, events and acts during childhood can also exert long-lasting effects; upon character and cause symptomatic breakdowns (Freud 1905, 1909, 1910, 1918). Since these discoveries of Freud, psychoanalysis has come a long way. We have come to realize that a strictly linear relationship between childhood and adulthood does not exist. We have accepted that our reconstructions of early childhood experiences lack certainty; this is especially true for the preverbal era of childhood. Concepts of *screen memory* (Freud 1899, 1901), *change of function* (Hartmann 1939), condensation of various levels of development, and *overdetermination* (Waelder 1936) have given us pause while feeling tempted towards genetic reductionism, especially of a conclusive and absolute kind. The debate on whether psychoanalysis unearths historical truth or merely constructs *narrative truth* (Spence 1982) captures some of the issues involved here. Matters have been rendered even more complex in light of the current controversy regarding psychoanalytic data being given or co-constructed, the latter being the crux of the intersubjective perspective (Dunn 1995).

However, such conundrum has not altogether ruled out the *genetic perspective* (Rapaport 1959) on character formation and psychopathology. Childhood is still seen as having a major formative impact upon adulthood. This continuity involves autonomous ego functions, talents, ego strengths, sublimations, and healthy identifications as well as conflicts, deficits, pathogenic fantasies, and effects of traumatic events. This last mentioned aspect brings us back to Freud, though we return with a richer armamentarium of observational skills, data collection, theory, and technique. Dr. Settlage's contribution is a shining example of this trend.

DR. SETTLAGE'S CONTRIBUTION

Dr. Settlage offers us developmental, phenomenological, and technical perspectives on the effects of early libidinal loss. Taking intellectual cues from Freud (1926), A. Freud (1946), Spitz (1965), Mahler (1966, 1971, 1974 and Schur (1966) and synthesizing them with his own long-standing empirical observations (Settlage et al. 1990, 1991, 1993) and clinical experience (Settlage 1973, 1989, 1992, 1993, 1994). Dr. Settlage suggests that the unfolding of a child's potential is dependent upon the releasing function of maternal availability and support. Without that, either the evolving self atrophies and becomes psychically marasmic or develops along pathological lines. The impact of maternal loss through death and desertion is quantitatively greater than through inattention and neglect, though the latter also have qualitatively similar effects upon the child.

One particular aspect of the resulting pathology Dr. Settlage focuses upon is the repression and subsequent non-assimilation of aggression in the functioning and structure of the core self and object representation. This leads to excessive dependency on external objects, turning of aggression against the self, depletion of assertive potential, inordinate separation anxiety, a childlike stance in life, and an exaggerated fear of death. Dr. Settlage goes on to illustrate this etiological and phenomenological portrait by presenting three case histories. Implicitly, he forwards a view of psychoanalytic technique suitable for such patients. This approach is unabashedly therapeutic in intent and incorporates elements of the "classical" as well as a developmentally informed perspective. Thus clarification, interpretation, and reconstruction find as prominent a place in Dr. Settlage's work as do support, affirmation, perceptual refueling, encouragement, provision of transitional objects, and active efforts at helping the patient master the effects of childhood loss.

Throughout all this, Dr. Settlage shows a sophisticated, evenhanded manner of conceptualizing and working. In discussing ontogenesis, he includes comments upon phylogenesis. In addressing experiential factors of childhood, he makes sure to acknowledge the hard-wired readiness of the brain for adaptation. In elucidating the interpersonal, he does not lose sight of the intrapsychic. And, in the realm of literature coverage too, he deftly integrates the older writings (Freud 1917, 1926, A. Freud 1946, Spitz 1964, 1965, Mahler 1966, 1971, 1974) with the contemporary (Emde 1980, Pine 1986, Schore 1994, Stern 1985). His clinical material also is inclusive. He presents both child and adult, as well as male and female, cases. He elucidates the effects of childhood object loss and adult suffering via transference rupture (due to the analyst's out-of-town move) to be in complex dialectical interchange with each other. Dr. Settlage's clinical material is convincing and his excellence as a therapist, an analyst, and a kind human being comes across loud and clear. All in all, I find his contribution to be impressive, deeply human, though provoking, and useful.

THE EXPERIENTIAL WORLD OF
MATERNALLY DEPRIVED INDIVIDUALS

I am in agreement with Dr. Settlage's symptomatic picture resulting from early deprivation. However, I feel that the following six
points need more attention than Dr. Settlage has given them.

Mental Pain

In Dr. Settlage's contribution there is less than optimal distinction
between the three types of affects (Freud 1926) that occur in
response to separation: mental pain, separation anxiety, and mourning. Mental pain especially escapes his attention. This is not
surprising since not only the affect is elusive but the literature
addressing it is meager. Freud (1926) introduced the concept in
psychoanalytic literature under the rubric of *Seelenshmerz* (literally,
soul-pain). He acknowledged that he knew very little about
this affect and fumbled in describing it. He referred to a child's
crying for his mother and evoked analogies to bodily injury
and loss of body parts. He also mentioned a sense of "longing"
and "mental helplessness" (pp. 171–172) as being components of
mental pain. In the "Project" he suggested that *Schmerz* (pain)
resulted form a marked increase in the quantity of stimuli impinging upon the mind. This caused "a breach in the continuity"
(1895b, p. 307) of the protective shield. Pain was a direct result
of such shock trauma. In *Mourning and Melancholia*, Freud related
pain to object loss and said that the complex of melancholia
behaved like "an open wound" (1917, p. 253). It was, however, not
until an addendum to *Inhibition, Symptoms and Anxiety* (1926, pp.
169–172) that Freud linked his economic explanations to his
object–related hypothesis regarding the origins of mental pain. He
suggested that where there is physical pain, an increase in narcissistic cathexis of the afflicted site occurs and the same is true or

mental pain. In illustrating his ideas through the situation of an infant separated from his mother, Freud implied that the object loss leading to mental pain occurred at a psychic level of ego-object non-differentiation. Weiss (1934) made this explicit by stating that:

> Pain arises when an injury—a break, so to speak, in the continuity—occurs within the ego . . . Love objects become, as we know, libidinally bound to the ego, as if they were parts of it. If they are torn away from it, the ego reacts as though it had sustained mutilation. The open wound thus produced in it is just what comes to the expression as mental pain (p. 12).

Thus was born the notion that mental pain is not an accompaniment of any object loss but only of the object loss that lead to an ego rupture. It is perhaps in this spirit subsequent analysts used words such as "pining" (Klein 1940, p. 360) and "longing" (Joffee and Sandler 1965, p. 156) in association with mental pain. They also resorted to somatic analogies and metaphors. Indeed, in mapping out the affective world, Pontalis (1981) placed pain "at the frontiers and juncture of body and psyche, of death and life" (p. 131). In a recent effort at bringing these and other scattered writings (Khan 1979, Joseph 1981, Kogan 1990) on this subject together (Akhtar 2000a), I stated:

> Mental pain consists of a wordless sense of self-rupture, longing, and psychic helplessness that is vague and difficult to convey to others. It usually follows the loss of a significant object or its abrupt refusal to meet one's anaclitic needs. This results in the laceration of an unconscious, fused self-object core of the self. Abruptly precipitated discrepancies between the actual and wished-for self-states add to the genesis of mental pain. Issues of hatred, guilt, moral masochism, as well as fantasies of being beaten can also be folded into the experience of

mental pain. The feeling is highly disturbing and is
warded off by psychic retreat, manic defense, induction of
pain into others and changing the form and function of
pain. Each of these can have a pathological or healthy
outcome depending upon the intrapsychic and social
context upon whether they ultimately permit mourning
to take place or not (p. 229).

Defenses against mental pain differ from those against anxiety
(Akhtar 2000a) and include manic defense. It is therefore of technical significance that mental pain be recognized in its specificity.
Dr. Settlage, in his clinical work, seems attuned to this affect but
it does not enter his theorizing.

Atrophy, Splitting, and Repression
of Aggression

Aggression mobilized by ruptures of early maternal care undergoes
more vicissitudes than repression, Dr. Settlage's preferred term,
encompasses. Of course, it can be repressed. It can also be split off
and directed at objects other than the mother (or the analyst). It
can be turned against the self, as Dr. Settlage acknowledges. It can
also fail to develop as a coherent phenomenon altogether. Those
who are very deprived and have little in the form of reliable
libidinal ties fail to develop the normal entitlement to be angry.
They lack a "healthy capacity for indignation" (Ambassador
Nathaniel Howell, personal communication, April 1996). Such is
frequently the case with schizoid and *as if* (Deutsch 1942) personalities. This is not repression; it is atrophy before occurrence,
so to speak. Indeed such atrophy, splitting and repression form a
hierarchy in the inner processing of early aggression in maternally
deprived individuals. And, this has technical implications insofar
as the analyst, in such cases, should not interpret the absence of
anger on the patient's part as defensive but empathize with the
horrid fact that the patient feels no right to feel angry at all!

Manic Defense

Dr. Settlage hints at other defenses, but I find his elucidation incomplete especially because it overlooks the concept of *manic defense* (Klein 1935, Winnicott 1935). Since this concept is not well know to the North American psychiatric and psychoanalytic readership, I will describe it in some detail. Klein (1935) described manic defense as a set of mental mechanisms aimed at protecting the ego from depressive as well as paranoid anxieties. She delineated many forms of *manic defense* and often used the term in its plural form. Essentially, manic defense attempts to deny the ego's "perilous dependence on its love objects" (p. 277) and the danger with which it is menaced from its internalized bad objects. Omnipotence, denial, and idealization are three constituents of manic defense. *Omnipotence* is utilized to control and master objects, but without genuine concern for them. *Denial* is aimed at erasing the awareness of dependence upon others. *Idealization* tenaciously retains an "all good" view of the world and oneself which, in turn, defends against guilty recognition of having injured others in fact or fantasy.

Winnicott (1935) emphasized that manic defense is intended to "deny the depressive anxiety that is inherent in emotional development, anxiety that belongs to the capacity of the individual to feel guilt, and also to acknowledge responsibility for instinctual experiences, and for the aggression in the fantasy that goes with individual experiences" (pp. 143–144). He outlined four components of manic defense (1) denial of internal reality, (2) flight to external reality from internal reality, (3) suspended animation, and (4) reversal of depressive feelings. The *denial of inner reality* involves a repudiation of internalized bad objects, but it can also send the good internal forces and objects into psychic exile. "Many who live normal and valuable lives do not feel they are responsible for the best that is in them" (p. 133). *Flight to external reality* involves frequent daydreaming, which interposes fantasy between the internal and external reality, as an intermediary step. Or, there might be an exploitation of sexuality and/or hypochondriasis for avoiding internal reality. In the *suspended animation* aspect of manic defense, omnipotent control of the bad internal objects stops all truly good relationships. The individual feels dead inside and the world appears still and colorless. Finally, manic defense involves the *reversal of depressive feelings* and use of exalted opposites (full as against empty, moving as against still, fast as against slow, light as against heavy, etc.) for reassurance. Manic defense also impacts on symbolism. Height and tallness, for instance, usually have phallic significance, but they might also allude to manic defense in operation. Balloons often signify breasts, but their lightness and playfulness might also be used as "contra-depressive symbols" (p. 136).

The use of manic defense is typical of individuals who dread sadness and are unable to mourn. They gloss over disturbing events with astonishing ease, keep busy, avoid aloneness, are fun-loving, have a large circle of friends, and are easily excitable. Many narcissistic, hypomanic, histrionic, and as-if personalities fit this picture. More to the point of Dr. Settlage's paper, manic defense is a frequent maneuver against pain and suffering associated with childhood object loss; it only later gets incorporated into character.

Exaggerated Fear of Death

Dr. Settlage refers to the exaggerated fear of death in individuals who have suffered actual or functional libidinal object loss during childhood. I agree with this observation. However, I think there is both a quantitative and qualitative difference in the fear of death experienced by normal persons and that felt by maternally deprived individuals. In the former, fear of death draws affective tributaries from deepest remnants of annihilation anxiety, fear of separation from love objects, castration fantasies, and the unconscious longing for eternal rest (Akhtar 1995a). In those who have experienced childhood loss, all these factors are operative. In addition, there is a repudiated pressure to identify with the dead mother (Green 1988) and become nothing (see also Lichtenstein 1963). Having, at times, been treated as inanimate by callously inattentive or enraged parents has also blurred their inner boundaries of animate and inanimate, and they fear the latter self will take their entire existence over. Finally, the despair at dying without having joyously lived is far more, as one would expect, than at expecting death after having lived well.

Disturbances in the Experience of Time

While Dr. Settlage hints at such patients staying childlike and hoping that their "all good" mothers will return, he does not emphasize enough how disruptive this attitude is to the patient's sense of time. These patient live in the past and/or in the future, never in the present. They wring their hands claiming that *if only* (Akhtar 1991, 1994, 1996) their childhood would have been better, they would be trouble-free today; this partial truth seems to mask their ongoing sadomasochism. Or they keep hoping that *someday* (Akhtar 1991, 1994, 1996) all their troubles will be over; often their *pathological hope* (Amati-Mehler and Argentieri 1989) contains the fantasy of *wunderglauben* (Angel 1932), that is, a dramatic event that will change their fate forever. *Malignant erotic transference* (Akhtar 1994) and interminable analyses often reflect such pathology.

Disturbances in Sexual Life

While I am aware that clinical presentations inevitable offer only selective material, I am still left with feeling that there is too little sex in Dr. Settlage's material. Give the early loss and the consequent object hunger, one would expect there to be sexual repercussions of it all. Kernberg (1975) points out that intense sexual

strivings may prematurely develop in a child to deny frustrated oral
dependent needs. He emphasizes that such development powerfully reinforces oedipal fears by pregenital fears of the mother.
Under these circumstances, a positive Oedipus complex is seriously interfered with. Adult sexuality is then characterized by
either sexualized dependency or prominent negative oedipal
trends. These manifest in greedy promiscuity and orally derived
homosexuality among men, and among women, in an intensified
penis envy, flight into promiscuity to deny penis envy, or a
sexualized search for the gratification of oral needs from an idealized mother, leading to homosexuality. In delineating the phenomenological profiles of various severe personality disorders, I
(Akhtar 1992) have consistently included the disturbances in their
sexual life.

WHAT CAN THE FATHER DO?

Dr. Settlage offers a disclaimer that he is using "mother" as a
shorthand for the early caretaker. And, he does include a few
comments regarding the father in two of his three cases. However,
this seems inoptimal. It fails to emphasize the father's profoundly
important role in the development of children. I have elsewhere
(Akhtar 1995) summarized this role in the following words:

> (1) By being a protective, loving, and collaborative part-
> ner to the mother, the father facilitates and enhances her
> ability to devote herself to the child. (2) By offering
> himself as a relatively neutral, ego-oriented, new object
> during the rapprochement subphase of separation-indi-
> viduation, the father provides the child with stability, a
> haven from conflict, and (in the case of a boy) and im-
> portant measure of *dis-identification* (Greenson 1968) from
> the mother. (3) By appearing on the evolving psychic
> horizon of the child as the romantic partner of the

mother, the father helps consolidate the child's capacity to experience, bear, and benefit from the triangular familial relationship and the conflicts attendant upon it. (4) By presenting himself as an admirable model for identification to his son and by reflecting the budding femininity of his daughter with restrained reciprocity, the father enriches his children's gender identity and gives direction to their later sexual object choices (Akhtar 1995b).

In the specific context of early libidinal loss, the father can have at least three kinds of impact: (1) By being supportive to a child whose mother has turned away (transiently, because of having just given birth to a new baby, or on a more sustained basis, due to chronic illness, for instance), the father can mitigate the potentially deleterious effects of the libidinal depletion of the mother–child tie. (2) By himself being unavailable the father can compound the child's sense of depletion in such circumstances. This can leave the child excessively tied to an empty mother, which thwarts separation–individuation. (3) Finally, if the father's love is too maternal in quality, it might help a deprived child initially but later rob the child of a prototype of mourning; the child feels what is lost can be readily found and thus bypasses the experience of hopelessness necessary for realistic ego growth.

There are gender-related issues here as well. A female child who is neglected by the mother might benefit by father's love at the preoedipal level but accrue horrible guilt at the oedipal level, especially if the father is overtly devaluing of the mother. A male child might not develop such guilt, although he might become excessively prone to homosexual desire. Gender identity is another area that might be differentially effected. A girl deprived by mother might experience greater difficulty in forming a feminine identity since that requires identifying with the "enemy." A boy might have lesser problems in this regard. While Dr. Settlage presents us both male and female cases, he does not comment upon these gender differences in the impact of maternal turning away.

DR. SETTLAGE'S TREATMENT TECHNIQUE

Dr. Settlage's analytic approach, as stated above, is unabashedly therapeutic. While it comprises the usual dose of empathic listening, deciphering of hidden messages, clarification, interpretation, and reconstruction, it also contains a robust dose of support, meeting of needs, provision of transitional objects (e.g., his gift to his patient, Ilana, at the time of their parting), perceptual refueling, judicious self-disclosure, and encouragement. To some, such admixture of interpretive and development-facilitating interventions would constitute a most reasonable approach. From Winnicott (1956, 1965) through Loewald (1960) and Stone (1961) to Pine (1999), one can find support of such a stance. On the other hand, it would be dishonest to deny that others (both within the contemporary ego-psychological approach as well as the Kleinian tradition) would not question Dr. Settlage's technique. His enormously impressive availability might appear to them as inability to bear patient's negative transferences. It might be regarded as a countertransference enactment to bypass the patient's rage at what has happened, and what cannot be done to repair that damage. Analysis, these critics of Dr. Settlage might say, does not work through the analyst's generosity and kindness.

I myself am on Dr. Settlage's side in this debate. Indeed in a recent elucidation of contemporary psychoanalytic technique, I (Akhtar 200b) have advocated an approach similar to his. Nonetheless, vis-à-vis some of his interventions (especially his giving a gift to his patient), I find it difficult to avoid joining the line of his critics.

CONCLUSION

Throughout this discussion, my message has been that manic defense is problematic and mourning is useful. Now it is time to give succinct rationale for these positions. Manic defense is problematic because it robs us of contact with our inner reality without which we cannot be truthful about ourselves. And, being truthful is a precondition of mental health (Bion 1967). Manic defense is therefore contrary to mental health and sooner or later needs to be worked through. Mourning is useful because it permits us to relinquish attachments and attitudes that have lost their realistic usefulness. It therefore facilitates growth and development. In the absence of mourning, we remain attached to early internal objects that are frustrating and often defensively idealized and the self-representations associated with them. Matters are complicated by the fact that such unmourned fragments of psyche are usually repressed. When this happens, not only are the internal objects sent into psychic exile, but we also lose the self-representations attached to those objects. We are thus depleted in our relatedness to the world and impoverished in our knowledge of ourselves. Lack of mourning makes the world bankrupt and the self amputated, a state of affairs captured in my poem "Mourning":

What happens to lost pets?
Do they become others' pets?
Do they have an accident and get killed?
Do they stop needing protection and start living by themselves?

What happens to old girlfriends?
Do they become others' girlfriends?
Do they have an accident and get pregnant?
Do they stop needing love and start living by themselves?

What happens to the parts of oneself
That go with each lost pet and each parted girlfriend?

REFERENCES

Akhtar, S. (1991). Three fantasies related to unresolved separation-individuation: a less recognized aspect of severe character pathology. In *Beyond the Symbiotic Orbit:*

Advances in Separation-Individuation Theory—Essays in Honor of Selma Kramer, M.D., ed. S. Akhtar and H. Parens, pp. 261–284. Hillsdale, NJ: The Analytic Press.

———. (1992) *Broken Structures: Severe Personality Disorders and their Treatment.* Northvale, NJ: Jason Aronson Inc.

———. (1994) Object constancy and adult psychopathology. *International Journal of Psycho-Analysis* 75:441–455.

———. (1995a). Aggression: theories regarding its nature and origins. In *Psychoanalysis: The Major Concepts*, ed. B.E. Moore and B.D. Fine, pp. 364–380. New Haven, CT: Yale University Press.

———. (1995b). *Quest for Answers: A Primer for Understanding and Treating Severe Personality Disorders.* Northvale, NJ: Jason Aronson Inc.

———. (1996). "Someday . . ." and "if only . . ." fantasies: pathological optimism and inordinate nostalgia as related forms of idealization. *Journal of the American Psychoanalytic Association* 44:723–753.

———. (2000a). Mental pain and the cultural ointment. *International Journal of Psycho-Analysis* 81:229–243.

———. (2000b). From schisms through synthesis to informed oscillation: an attempt at integrating some diverse aspects of psychoanalytic technique. *Psychoanalytic Quarterly* 69:265–288.

Amati-Mehler, J. and Argentieri, S. (1989). Hope and hopelessness: a technical problem? *International Journal of Psycho-Analysis* 70:295–304.

Angel, A. (1932). Einige bemerkungen uber den optimismus. *International Zeitschrift of Psychoanalysis* 20:191–199.

Bion, W. (1967). *Second Thoughts.* New York: Jason Aronson Inc.

Deutsch, H. (1942). Some forms of emotional disturbance and their relationship to schizophrenia. *Psychoanalytic Quarterly* 11:301–312.

Dunn, J. (1995). Intersubjectivity in psychoanalysis: a critical review. *International Journal of Psycho-Analysis* 76:723–738.

Emde, R. (1980). Toward a psychoanalytic theoty of affect II: emerging models of emotional development in infancel. In *The Course of Life: Psychoanalytic Contributions Towards Understanding Personality Development, Volume 1: Infancy and Early Childhood*, ed. S.I. Greenspan and G.H. Pollock. DHHS Publication No. (ADM) 80-786.

Freud A. (1946). *The Ego and the Mechanisms of Defence.* New York: International Universities Press.

Freud S. (1895a). Studies on hysteria (with J. Breuer). *Standard Edition* 2:1–323.

———. (1895b). Project for a scientific psychology. *Standard Edition* 1:295–398.

———. (1896). Specific aetiology of hysteria. *Standard Edition* 3:163–168.

———. (1899). Screen memories. *Standard Edition 3:301–323*

———. (1901). Childhood memories and screen memories. *Standard Edition* 6:43–52.

———. (1905). Fragment of an analysis of case of hysteria. *Standard Edition* 7:135–243.

———. (1909). A phobia in a five-year-old boy. *Standard Edition* 10:5–149.

———. (1910). A special type of object choice made by men. *Standard Edition* 11:163–175.

———. (1917). Mourning and melancholia. *Standard Edition* 14:237–258.

———. (1918). From the history of an infantile neurosis. *Standard Edition* 17:1–122.

———. (1926). Inhibitions, symptoms, and anxiety. *Standard Edition* 20:77–174.

Green, A. (1988). The dead mother. In *On Private Madness*. New Haven, CT: International Universities Press.

Hartmann, H. (1939). *Ego Psychology and the Problem of Adaptation.* Trans. D. Rapaport. New York: International Universities Press.

Joffee, W. G. and Sandler J. (1965). Pain, depression, and individuation. In *From Safety to Superego*, ed. J. Sandler, pp. 154–179. New York: Guilford.

Joseph, B. (1981). Towards the experiencing of psychic pain. In *Psychic Equilibrium and Psychic Change: Selected Papers of Betty Joseph*, ed. M. Feldman and E. B. Spillius, pp. 88–97. London: Routledge.

Kernberg, O.F. (1975). *Borderline Conditions and Pathological Narcissism.* New York: Jason Aronson Inc.

Khan, M.M.R. (1979). Fram masochism to psychic pain. In *Alienation in Perversions*, pp. 210–218. New York: International Universities Press.

Klein, M. (1935). A contribution to the psychogenesis of manic-depressive states. In *Love, Guilt and Reparation and Other Works 1921–1945*, pp. 262–289. New York: Free Press, 1992.

———. (1940). Mourning and its relation to manic-depressive states. In *The Writings of Melanie Klein, Volume I: Love, Guilt and Reparation*, pp. 344–369. London: Hogarth, 1975.

Kogan, I. (1990). A journey to pain. *International Journal of Psycho-Analysis* 71:629–640.

Lichtenstein, H. (1963). The dilemma of human identity: notes on self-transformation, self-objectivation, and metamorphosis. *Journal of the American Psychoanalytic Association* 11:173–223.

Loewald, H. (1960). On the therapeutic action of psychoanalysis. *International Journal of Psycho-Analysis* 41:16–33.

Mahler, M.S. (1966). Notes on the development of basic moods: the depressive affect. In *The Selected Papers of Margaret S. Mahler, Volume 2*, pp. 59–76. New York: Jason Aronson Inc., 1979.

———. (1971). A study of the separation-individuation process and its possible application to borderline phenomena in the psychoanalytic situation. In *The Selected Papers of Margaret S. Mahler, Volume 2*, pp. 169–187. New York: Jason Aronson Inc., 1979.

———. (1974). Symbiosis and individuation: the psychological birth of the human infant. In *The Selected Papers of Margaret S. Mahler, Volume 2*, pp. 149–165. New York: Jason Aronson Inc., 1979.

Pine, F. (1986). The "symbiotic" phase in the light of current infancy research. *Bulletin of the Menninger Clinic* 50:564–569.

———. (1999). *Diversity and Direction in Psychoanalytic Theory and Technique.* New Haven, CT: Yale University Press.

Pontalis, J.B. (1981). *Frontiers in Psychoanalysis.* New York: International Universities Press.

Rapaport, D. (1959). The structure of psychoanalytic theory. *Psychological Issues.* 6:39–72.

Schore, A.N. (1994). *Affect Regulation and the Origin of the Self.* Hillsdale, NJ: Lawrence Erlbaum.

Schur, M. (1966). *The Id and the Regulatory Principles of Mental Functioning.* New York: International Universities Press.

Settlage, C.F. (1973). Cultural values and the superego in late adolescence. *Psychoanalytic Study of the Child,* 27:74–92.

———. (1989). The interplay of therapeutic and developmental process in the treatment of children: an application of contemporary object relations theory. *Psychoanalytic Inquiry* 9:375–396.

———. (1992). Psychoanalytic observations on adult development in life and in the therapeutic relationship. *Psychoanalysis and Contemporary Thought* 15:349–374.

———. (1993). Therapeutic process and developmental process in the restructuring of object and self constancy. *Journal of the American Psychoanalytic Association* 41:473–492.

———. (1994). On the contribution of separation-individuation theory to psychoanalysis: developemnt, psychopathology, and treatment. In *Mahler and Kohut: Perspectives on Development, Psychopathology, and Technique,* ed. S. Kramer and S. Akhtar, pp. 17–52. Northvale, NJ: Jason Aronson Inc.

Settlage, C.F., Bemesderfer, S., Rosenthal, J., Afterman, J., and Spielman, P.M. (1991). The appeal cycle in early mother–child interaction: the nature and implication of a finding from developmental research. *Journal of the American Psychoanalytic Association* 39:987–1014.

Settlage, C.F., Rosenthal, J., Spielman, P.M., Gassner, S., Afterman, J., Bemesderfer, S. and Kolodny, S. (1990). An exploratory study of mother–child interaction during the second year of life. *Journal of the American Psychoanalytic Association* 38:705–731.

Settlage, C.F., Silver, D.H., Hart, K. and Nelson, K. (1993). Developmental process: mother–child and father–child interaction during the second year of life. In *Family, Self, and Society: Toward a New Agenda for Family Research,* ed. P.A. Cowan, D. Field, D. Hanse, E. Skolnick, and G. E. Swanson, pp. 363–384. Hillsdale, NJ: Lawrence Erlbaum.

Spence, D.P. (1982). *Narrative truth and Historical Truth*. New York: W. W. Norton.

Spitz, R. (1964). The derailment of dialogue: stimulus overload, action cycles, and the completion of gradient. *Journal of the American Psychoanalytic Association* 12:752–775.

———. (1965). *The First Year of Life*. New York: International Universities Press.

Stern, D.N. (1985). *The Interpersonal World of the Infant*. New York: Basic Books.

Stone, L. (1961). *The Psychoanalytic Situation*. New York: International Universities Press.

Waelder, R. (1936). The principle of multiple function: observations on multiple determination. *Psychoanalytic Quarterly* 5:45–62.

Weiss, E. (1934). Bodily pain and mental pain. *International Journal of Psycho-Analysis* 15:1–13.

Winnicott, D.W. (1935). The manic defense. In *Through Paediatrics to Psycho-Analysis: Collected Papers*, pp. 129–144. New York: Brunner/Mazel, 1992.

———. (1956). The antisocial tendency. In *Through Paediatrics to Psycho-Analysis*, pp. 306–315. London: Tavistock, 1958.

———. (1965). *The Maturational Processes and the Facilitating Environment*. New York: International Universities Press.

6

TECHNICAL PROBLEMS IN ANALYZING THE MOURNING PATIENT

Herbert Schlesinger, M.D.

". . . gradual growing away from the maternal state of symbiosis, of one-ness with the mother, is a lifelong mourning process." (Mahler 1972, p. 333)

I have used this aphorism of Margaret Mahler to introduce my chapter in recognition of her original contributions to the understanding of mourning in developmental terms. Mahler, together with her co-workers and students, laid the groundwork for our current views, leaving it to coming generations to fill in the details.

The developmental point of view is well represented on this platform by analysts who have had firsthand experience in working with children at all stages of development. Sadly, my analytic training, like my earlier clinical training, did not include exposure to children. I have not had occasion to analyze a child since it was a matter of personal survival, when it was urgent that I figure out what the bigger kids had in mind for me. Since then, I have watched children and listened to them, and I have listened to my betters about them, so that now my claim to expertise in child development and child analysis is at least as strong as that of a Catholic priest to offer marital counseling. Still, in deference to what some might consider insufficient standing, I will approach my topic from a phenomenological point of view, drawing only on my experience in analyzing adults and supervising candidates.

THE UBIQUITY OF MOURNING

Let me begin by recalling some banalities: First: Loss is the single universal and essential human experience. Death and taxes are inescapable; eventual loss of substance and of life itself is the lot of us all. Yet consider, this stark realization is not pessimistic, for without the ability to appreciate loss it is not possible to experience gain. Loss, or more precisely, the ability to recognize loss, to accept it and to let go, is the necessary condition for growth and maturation. Appreciating loss is a corollary of being aware of separateness. It is also the essential discrimination for the testing of reality. You realize, of course, that in my apostrophizing of loss I have merely turned on its head the Mahlerian conception of the importance of object-constancy for developing a sense of self and for normal growth and development.

A second banality: Coming to terms with limitations, which is to say coming to terms with what is not one, or with what one is not, also implies becoming reconciled with surrendering infinitude, an aspect of surrendering omnipotence. When so engaged, one is well on the way toward wisdom, or at least to reasonably effective reality testing.[1]

Mahler's poetic statement that mourning is a lifelong process is literally true for the patient in analysis. I hasten to add that I

---

[1] I will use the term mourning broadly so that it should be understood to include grieving, the initial reaction of recognition of loss, and the rest of the process of working through loss.

do not mean to imply that analysis ought to be a lifelong process, but rather that for our patients, loss and the necessity to come to terms with it may be a daily occurrence. How can that be? Fortunately, losing a significant other through death while in analysis is not a common occurrence. But progress in self-understanding often does lead to giving up a relationship that one has outgrown, or accepting that the nature of a relationship has changed, and while that process implies growth, it can also be experienced as loss and may be difficult to bear. And there are other occasions during analysis when the patient either experiences loss, or more frequently ought to be able to experience loss, but defends himself against the experience as a way to avoid the pain involved.

Let us agree then that mourning is a normal and adaptive reaction to loss. In the clinical situation, it ought to be experienced for what it is and what it is about. We could say that it is one of the responsibilities of the analyst to protect the mourning process so that it may proceed toward its natural ending. The mourning process may need protection both against the patient's efforts to minimize pain by denying loss, thus seeming to make mourning superfluous, and protection also from problems the analyst may have in dealing with loss. My major thesis is that the phenomena associated with mourning are to be seen and appreciated in every analysis, but they may be minimized or overlooked by both analyst and patient either out of ignorance or for defensive reasons. Each of these instances may involve different technical considerations and so I will address them separately.

ARE THERE TECHNICAL IMPLICATIONS ABOUT MOURNING?

To speak of technical implications of mourning might arouse the fear that I am about to advocate interpreting the process of mourning itself. Let me disavow that notion at once. Analyzing, at least in its narrowest and most specific sense, interpreting, is a form of explaining; we intend to inform the patient about the larger meaning of what is going on. Interpreting is our way of explaining, either by reducing a complicated phenomenon to simpler components or by revealing the complexity of a seemingly simple matter, or both. But mourning, like other normal processes, does not need explaining, at least not while it is going on. Sometimes explaining can get in the way. For a comic example, please visualize the *New Yorker* cartoon that showed a young couple on a mountaintop. It featured the dismay on the young woman's face as her callow boyfriend expatiated on the meteorology of the beautiful sunset they had climbed so far to see. It is much the same in an analysis. After all, neither sunsets nor mourning need explaining in order to appreciate them. This occasion is not the only instance, of course, when the proper analytic attitude is identical with the proper human attitude, that is deference, respect, and simple appreciation for the integrity of an experience.[2]

But there are technical considerations that derive from the analyst's responsibility to protect the mourning process. It often is painful to recognize that one has lost something precious, even when the loss is the unavoidable "dark side" of long-sought relief. For an example, I will generalize from examples many analysts could relate:

Case 1

Consider the experience of a woman who, with the help of analysis and after a long and expensive legal battle, has

---

[2]This identity may exist from the outset, for instance from the first hello or handshake. When the analyst believes the analytic attitude must diverge sharply from the ordinary human or socially conforming attitude, he must be ready to justify the deviation in terms of the necessities of analytic technique; it cannot be excused merely as a stylistic or analytic mannerism.

finally won a divorce from an abusive and vengeful husband. Her relief is palpable, but the anticipated joy seems muted, attenuated by an unexpected sadness, tears she cannot understand. She is willing to attribute her mood to weariness from the long struggle; was it all worth it? Only slowly does she recall that over the months of analyzing her attachment to the abusive husband, she had felt flashes of anticipatory loneliness. She had foreseen the possibility of feeling bereft when finally divorced. She had fearfully tried to balance the humiliation of remaining in an abusive marriage against the fear of being alone, the horror of not being married, of losing her identity as proper matron in society, of being "cut loose to drift." And even though it was she who was sick of abuse and wanted the divorce, she would berate herself for being a failure at "wife," the only role life had trained her for. She thought she had come to terms with "all that," only to find that from time to time she felt as if her worst fears had all come true. But would she really want to be back in the situation from which she had just escaped?

Analysts will recognize this common syndrome and most will conclude that these mixed feelings do not indicate that the analytic work was defective but rather that it was merely sufficient to get the patient to this point. It is "normal," that is to say expectable, for the patient to experience the loss again and again and to mourn and work through it repeatedly. Analysts will again recall Mahler's aphorism that mourning is a lifelong process and will draw from it the implication that no significant relationship is ever given up totally. Pfeffer (1993), in his interviews of former analysands, demonstrated how easily transference can be revived. And many of us have had the experience of a surge of sadness as, for instance, we enjoy contemplating a painting that once we enjoyed with another who is no longer with us.

Loss is painful and so is grieving and mourning, especially on occasions when there seems to be no social support for expressing such feelings openly; then one feels silly or self-indulgent and fears one may be embarrassing others and imposing on their patience. Many of our patients, like the rest of us, attempt to mitigate the pain of loss or the secondary social discomfort either by denying or minimizing the loss or by suppressing the processes nature has devised to deal with it. We tend to admire those who can keep a stiff upper lip and get on with it. There is a technical issue contained in these observations. It is essential that the analyst be familiar with the natural history of loss and of mourning. As the example above illustrates, significant loss is never fully expunged, while mourning is episodic and is not done once and for all time. Mourning recurs in waves, and as with all emotions, episodes rise to a peak and then dissipate. This phasic quality should not be confused with intermittent "resistance" against recognizing loss or against mourning. The distinction may be subtle at times, but it is an essential one. It would be better, technically, to err on the side of assuming normality, for to interpret the subsidence of an episode of sadness wrongly as resistance is likely to induce guilt in the patient for not being sincerely sorrowful. It can also be considered "normal" for the patient to attempt to mitigate the pain and to dose the mourning; not all such instances of defense require interpretation. Sometimes, an empathic observation such as, "It's hard when waves of sadness come over you," can provide support both for the patient allowing himself to feel the pain and for his reluctance to do so. An element of resistance may be present, of course, but without any implication of pathology and without obligating the analyst to "do something about it."

THE SEVERAL CONTEXTS
OF MOURNING

There are three contexts in which the analyst can expect to encounter mourning. The first is obvious, the second perhaps less so, and the third, which will occupy most of my attention, may at first even seem counterintuitive:

1. When the patient suffers the loss of a significant other;
2. When the patient loses a part of the self (e.g., a body part), an aspect of the self (e.g., a job), or a symptom; and
3. When the patient has resolved some issue of analytic importance sufficiently so that the ensuing change carries with it an intimation that the analysis will someday end and the relationship with the analyst will be severed.

We might think of this last context as anticipatory mourning, which of course in a realistic sense it is. But to view it so might lead us to overlook the immediacy of the feeling and the necessity to deal with it now, not to put it off until the someday when actual separation will occur.

Mourning the Loss of an "Other"

Since occasions of actual object loss are easy to recognize and may seem most straightforward for the analyst to deal with, I will focus on one of the major sources of technical difficulty. When a death of a parent occurs or when a spouse or equivalent dies or leaves, the stage is set for expectable reactions of grief and mourning. If the patient attempts to minimize the pain of loss through denial and avoidance, these efforts will be obvious. But for the seasoned analyst as well as the young one, there are some expectable intrusions on the proper treatment of the mourning patient that are not necessarily related to defensive efforts of the patient.

Defensiveness in the Analyst against
Mourning in the Patient

Among the forces that may interfere with the analyst's ability to discriminate whether he should intervene technically or allow the mourning process to continue unimpeded, of course, are transference of the analyst and his countertransference. The intrusions may take several forms. Some clinicians have difficulty tolerating the seeming passivity of remaining in a posture of witnessing; they feel impelled to intervene, to "do something." More common, perhaps, is the wish to spare our loved ones, including our patients and ourselves, pain of any kind, and in particular, prolonged pain, and we may feel impelled to alleviate our distress by intervening to ameliorate their suffering. It takes great discipline to allow a patient (or a loved one) to experience the processes of grieving and mourning fully and to appreciate, and help them appreciate, the importance of doing so. The tendency to interpret inappropriately at such times, or even to offer unneeded support, perhaps better called by its right name, "meddling," may be almost irresistible for the analyst who has also become attached to his patient and for whom empathy has drifted too close to identification. For example:

Case 2

The patient was a woman of early middle age who, after several years of analysis had managed to understand and overcome a lifelong tendency to alienate persons whom she had first cultivated and then feared would disappoint her "when she really needed them." She had met a man at her office who came in from the field from time to time. They took to each other and often would have lunch when he visited. Matters never progressed past that point, but the patient entertained fantasies that this man might be "Mr. Right"; indeed their meetings were mutually satisfying. She did not dare to find out if this man was married, as indeed he was. His attentions to her had always been friendly but correct so he gave her no obvious occasion to ask the fearful question. The analyst had anticipated that her hopes would be dashed, and had fantasized warning her to lower her expectations, but he could not think of a way to do so without putting a pin in her balloon. One day at lunch the man casually mentioned that he would have to leave time to pick out an anniversary gift for his wife. The patient was stunned and could recall nothing further about the lunch. In her subsequent analytic sessions she was mostly silent, sad, and hopeless: "What is the use of all this when the meaning has gone out of my life." The analyst realized he felt guilty for not having protected her and now wanted to make up for his perceived failure by easing her pain. Realizing that his own investment was excessive, he controlled his impulse to intervene and did not interfere with the patient's despair, but instead repeatedly acknowledged her pain. Only when she started to blame herself for letting herself fall in love when she should have realized that he wasn't really interested in her did he address her self-blaming (and implicitly blaming him) as defensive, as a way to divert herself from experiencing the pain of the loss. He added that even though she had contributed to her disillusionment through self-deception, and even though her expectations were inflated by fantasy, her involvement in it was real and the disappointment was still painful. His approach, as always, was to emphasize what her defensive maneuvers were intended to do for her, to moderate the pain she was feeling, rather than in the way supervisors often hear young analysts accuse patients of resisting, for example, "You are afraid to go deeper," or "You are trying to prevent further understanding." His intention, in bringing her back to the pain, was to help the patient discover that she could bear the vulnerability that she had always feared, a fear that for so long had kept her defended against intimacy. He wanted her to be able to discover that she could stand the pain and could work through the sense of loss. He understood this fantasized affair as equivalent to the adolescent crushes and disappointments that her neurosis had precluded and that she belatedly was experiencing a bit of once-stalled development that analysis had reopened for her. Her initial reaction to the analyst's efforts were to become furious with him, but soon enough she could acknowledge that she had not been destroyed and she was even pleased to discover that she could even look forward to the next visit of her friend.

Transference and countertransference may also interfere with the analyst's appreciation of the patient's experience in other ways. It is not uncommon that an analyst who has personal reasons to avoid mourning will become impatient or bored with the patient's "endless" complaints of loss. The analyst may tend to withdraw until the patient stops, or may "interpret" vigorously in a covert effort to shut the patient up. For defensive reasons, the patient may even invite such mistreatment by blaming himself for "carrying on" unnecessarily and boring the analyst.

As an aside, analysts must resist the common tendency of clinicians to "pathologize" the phenomena they want to highlight for the patient. It seems to be an aspect of a general tendency, (perhaps another instance of analyst's transference to the patient) to emphasize what is wrong with the patient and to ignore what is right. By commenting only on pathology, on flaws in reasoning or missing or distorted feelings, clinicians inadvertently subscribe to B.F. Skinner's operant conditioning paradigm: behavior that is ignored tends to drop away. The strategy may be effective if the target behavior is the naughtiness of unruly kids; if you don't pay any attention to it, it likely will stop. But it can be ruinous for the analysis if the analyst remains unresponsive when patients speak of enjoyment, satisfaction, or progress. By paying attention only to pathology, they effectively may indicate to the patient that they are not interested in hearing about what the patient considers to be progress.

Of course, this last observation is especially applicable to mourning. Since the experience is painful, patients may need encouragement to allow mourning to continue through its normal course. Like all emotions, mourning is episodic and the episodes have a limited duration. Patients who are fearful about losing control or are fearful that they may never stop crying may need to hear from the analyst that they do not need to interrupt this emotion or control it. As is often the case, hearing the truth may be encouragement enough.

Reactions to Loss of Parts of the Self

Mourning is the expectable response to loss in general, not just the kinds of losses analysts give the special name "object loss." A sense of loss also may be experienced when parts of the self have changed as a result of analysis. To the patient, a symptom, particularly a chronic one, may have assumed some of the qualities of an object, or in brief, may have acquired "object quality." The symptom may have been painful, embarrassing, and restrictive, such as attachment to an abusive spouse or a shameful obsession, something one dearly wants to be rid of.

The object quality of an obsolescent aspect of the self , that is, an inhibition or symptom, does not generally become obvious until analysis has rendered the symptom dynamically and economically redundant. Then it begins to lose its saliency in the patient's economy and may disappear completely. The patient may experience its diminution or absence with an acute sense of loss. He may reproach the analyst for taking away an "old friend," a dependable ally, and find it hard to conceive how life might go on without the symptom that had until now been an unwelcome fixture in his life. Until now he has had to plan his life around the inhibition or around the inconvenience of the special practices demanded of him by the symptom. Now, and to that same degree, life is emptier; he no longer has to think about IT, "but what else should I think about?" One patient who was losing her taste for her former flamboyant lifestyle accused the analyst, "You have taken away my grand opera and left me with only plain vanilla."

The process of working through the implications of the loss of a symptom resembles the process of mourning the loss of a significant other, though it is likely to be briefer. But unless the analyst is prepared to witness such experiences, the patient may attempt to hide them and thus will forego the opportunity to work through all of the implications of change. For example:

Case 3

The patient was a young lawyer who had a severe work inhibition that manifested itself in creating ingenious obstacles that served to prevent him from writing briefs. Somehow, essential files would be lost and would turn up at the last moment, often under a pile of unrelated documents on his desk. As the analysis progressed, the patient came to understand the significance of his behavior as a way of arousing anxiety in his superiors about whether he would get his work done. In that way, he could force them to keep him in mind and get even with them for their perceived ignoring of him. He began to appreciate the self-destructiveness of his behavior and started to modify it. As he did so, he began to feel waves of resentment. Wasn't the analyst manipulating him to conform to his old-fashioned values, the old Puritan ethic? He felt deprived, but in a way he could not at first articulate. His associations led to earlier times of being deceived and he settled finally on feeling that once again he was being tricked out of something he valued, just as when he was cheated by an older, cannier schoolmate who had talked him into trading a rare but crumpled baseball card for two common but shinier ones. Further associations led to recalling the traumatic loss of a transitional object, by then a tattered, filthy, crib blanket, his "Blanky" that was his constant companion as a tot and without which he could not nap. Since he had outgrown his baby furniture, his mother decided to redo his bedroom and with the new furniture came new bed linens. "Blanky" vanished that day, and the child could not be consoled by the new blanket that was offered as substitute. He searched in vain for he was told only that he must have misplaced it. As he accused the analyst of stealing away the best way he knew to keep his superiors off balance, it suddenly came to him that "Blanky" must have been trashed by his beloved grandmother, a live-in baby-sitter. She had tried to discourage his searching for it by sneering, "What do you want with that dirty thing, you're a big boy and big boys don't drag around rags." He realized then that in some way he must always have known its fate, but could not let himself be furious with his grandmother, who was a much more constant source of comfort than his ambitious and distant mother. Then he could connect his suppressed certainty about the rape of "Blanky" with the wish to get even with his boss by hiding essential papers. Mourning for the lost symptom had become conflated with mourning for lost "Blanky" and the restored connection began to free the patient from the compulsion to reenact his revengeful and self-destructive fantasies at work.

In this instance, the patient announced clearly how he reacted to the loss of his symptom, but that is a sometime event; the analyst cannot count on such validation. Much of the time, the indication that loss is being experienced is not clearly identified as such, and the defenses against experiencing mourning may be quite subtle. The main evidence may be negative: the absence of pleasure or the short-lived sense of relief following the removal of a tedious burden. The patient may seem glum without obvious reason, may seem detached or show loss of interest when the changes in his inner life and external situation might naively suggest that it would be more fitting if he would display unalloyed excitement at the range of new possibilities.

Mourning as Part of the Response to Therapeutic Change

By far the commonest instances of mourning in analysis are also those that are most likely to be overlooked both by analyst and patient. They are the occasions when the patient is changing as a function of the analyzing. Does that sound contradictory? Are occasions of analytic change not rare events, so rare that some wonder if they occur at all? No, actually moments of analytic change occur frequently, as often as the analyst offers a correct, well-timed interpretation. The problem is not the rarity of moments of change, but the failure of the analyst to recognize that his interpretation has affected the patient. Rather than following up and prolonging the state of flux or ambiguity that always follows a correct and well-timed interpretation, the analyst, having shot his bolt, relaxes and allows the altered neurotic structure to repair itself, letting the induced change dissipate (Schlesinger 1995). If the analyst would follow up and interpret both the patient's immediate confused mixture of positive and defensive reactions to the interpretation, the full reaction would be allowed to flower. The patient would then become more clearly aware of the complexity of his reaction and could start to tease apart the confused mixture of surprise, if not shock, relief, perhaps even a smidgen of pleasure, and also anxiety and dismay. Fearfully, he may ask, "Why am I feeling all this, is it all right, am I falling apart?" and resentment, "What are you doing to me?" Obviously, not all of these elements of reaction will be seen quite so clearly in every instance, and they tend to be seen successively rather than all at once. But the analyst who is alerted to expect such a response to interpretation will sense the most immediate and salient emotional reaction as well as the defensive tactics the patient invokes to contain it. He will respond so as to impede the process of reversion, as the patient tries to repair the damaged neurosis. When the analyst follows up assiduously, he may slow down, delay, or preclude the natural defensive reaction to immediately restore the *status quo ante*. When the state of post-interpretation flux is prolonged even briefly in this way, the change is allowed to persist, and the patient has a little time to adapt to it, to make room for it and eventually, for the change to become structuralized.

While I have described this process of following-up previously (Schlesinger 1995), I did not focus particularly on mourning as an aspect of the reaction to imminent change. After all, we regard change as desirable, while the aura of implication around the term *mourning* has the dull glow of finality, a terminal condition from which there is no return, only resignation. But I am afraid we are stuck with the term, just as we are stuck with the dismal term *termination*, with all its funereal implications.[3] But for our

---

[3]But let us not resign ourselves to the inevitability of several other objectionable terms such as the oxymoron "pathological mourning, " and the

patient in psychoanalysis, desirable as release from the bonds of inhibition or compulsion may be in fantasy, when change occurs, some of its implications are frightening. For every change involves loss as well as gain, and thus occasions of change expectably will also be occasions for mourning.

In addition to the sense of loss attributable to the change in the familiar sense of self, there is the inescapable awareness that further progress will lead inevitably to the end of the analysis. While at the outset of analysis, the patient likely wished devoutly that it would end sooner rather than later, once the patient becomes fully engaged it may seem impossible for him to think of life without it.

The analytic process can be construed as a succession of episodes of varying duration during which the patient works on

---

weaker epithets, "displaced mourning," and "pseudo mourning." Why are these usages objectionable? Because they assume there is such a "thing" as mourning; or to put it more precisely, that mourning is a condition that one could describe with a noun. With a sprinkling of adjectives we could then specify subtypes of the condition of mourning, some of which are so far from desirable that they almost qualify as diseases. But mourning is not a condition, it is a process; it doesn't have subtypes. We would do better to think that there are many ways to mourn and there are many ways to avoid mourning. Each of these ways must be understood by the clinician in its own terms rather than in the way it fails to meet the standard for ideal mourning the clinician might have in mind. They must be understood in terms of what the patient is trying to experience and what he is trying to avoid experiencing. We must ask what does it do for the patient to go about mourning in this way or what does it do for him to avoid mourning in this way. We must try to understand what the patient gains from his efforts, not just what it costs. It is essential that we understand what the patient would like to hold on to in the memory of the object and what he would prefer to put aside. What makes letting go so difficult, what else is put at risk by saying goodbye?

Perhaps I have alluded to a sort of clinical disease. But, more accurately, it should be considered a "disease" of clinicians; one we might refer to as "hardening of the categories." We tend to pathologize patient behavior we disapprove of, give it a bad name, and at least implicitly, urge our patients to stop doing it. We would do better to try to understand it than to banish it.

issues that sooner or later are "resolved" to some degree, that is the patient has gone as far as he can with it for the time being. At such times, the patient's absorption in the issue wanes, and he may seem to be a bit uncomfortable about feeling at loose ends. It may be less noticeable that he also is having some mixed feelings, including a degree of pleasure that he has achieved something, even though he may not know just what. It may perhaps be more obvious that he seems worried, but it may not be obvious that the worry is connected to the feeling of pleasure. The problem is that the patient is experiencing a sense of loss, though he probably will not identify it as such, for every achievement in analysis carries with it an "intimation of mortality," that is, success brings with it the fear that if there is much more of this "progress" the analysis will be over and then I will have to give up the analyst too.

For some patients, the fear of loss of the analyst as a consequence of achievement may be conscious or close enough to it that the patient tends to hide or minimize that he has achieved something, indeed the patient may not even let himself realize fully that some positive change has occurred. How often do we hear from our patients that others in the patient's life remark on improvements the patient has never reported and even seems to have been unaware of?

Certain patients believe they must deny or minimize any positive change lest the analyst get the idea that the patient has "had enough" and is ready for discharge, that is, can safely be abandoned. Some of these patients have the characterological conviction that only suffering makes them eligible for attention. They do not deserve care and have no right to expect that the analyst would be interested in them if they were free of symptoms. They have great difficulty in grasping the idea that they could remain in analysis simply because they want to and because they find it useful. Oddly enough, they would have to accept that they could stay in analysis indefinitely, if only they would want to do so, in order to consider the idea of ending electively.

The analyst who has not yet come to recognize these phenomena will not generally be helped by the patient, for patients do not generally try to make the nature of the problem clear. Indeed, for the patient who is concerned about eventual abandonment, clarity would not seem desirable. It is a bit like fearing to mention the word *cancer* when one goes for a physical exam, lest the doctor search for and find it. Rather than describing any of the phenomena I have just detailed, the patient may show irritation, hypersensitivity, resentment, and suspicion and no longer feel like "working"; he would rather keep secret the fact that the symptom had remitted or that things were going better at work or home, or that he had slept through the night or had enjoyable intercourse. For if the analyst would get wind of these improvements, the patient quickly would be eased out of analysis. A stalemate may occur, ironically triggered by unacknowledged progress.

The patient's experience when reacting to the anticipated loss of the analyst is complicated. Strictly speaking analytically, of course, there is no such thing as an anticipated loss. While the ostensible object, that is, the analyst, whose eventual loss is feared is actually present, in fantasy he is experienced as already gone. It is an experience that is difficult for the patient to explain to himself, and it is even more difficult to articulate convincingly to the analyst or others because it is so at odds with the evidence of his senses. It is akin to the problem of experiencing the analyst as a malignant transference figure while at the same time knowing cognitively that he couldn't be entirely so, and all the while trusting him enough to tell him these dire fears.

The sense of impending object loss, like all symptoms, can be viewed as a form of memory, a revival of an actual (or fantasized, e.g., oedipal) loss, and ironically, often represents an effort to prevent a loss that has already occurred. More precisely, since we are considering a fantasized loss, the patient is attempting to prevent the repetition of a loss that didn't occur in the first place. However, the fear that he will lose the analyst is really felt, and the patient must attempt to rationalize it even though the rationalization conflicts with the patient's experience of the analyst as one who is here now and who would not actually abandon him. The experience can be viewed as the actualization of the split between the transference object and the analyst. The patient's sense of reality inevitably is strained by the conflict between his cognitive and emotional experiences, and that secondary disjunction is also embarrassing and painful, a state that is most easily be expressed by silence.

The analyst must be aware that the patient's irritation and other dysphorias I mentioned earlier may be attributable as much to the discomfort about the equivocal transference experience as to the sense of loss itself. The analyst must be sensitive to the complexity of the patient's experience and not attempt to simplify it prematurely by interpreting it if, for the moment, the patient is defensively invested in maintaining the complexity and needs time to work through the emotional muddle. Here is an example:

Case 4

A young woman had been in analysis for over a year and had made a good deal of therapeutic progress in terms of relief of one of her presenting complaints. Now she was no longer so terribly shy. Formerly, much as she would have liked to be free and easy in social situations, she would become tongue-tied if approached by a man. She was angry and bitter about her inhibition and had avoided gatherings of her peers. Now to her delight, she found that she could converse with men in a way that, while still shy, was endearingly so rather than discomforting. She had other problems, of course, and her partial success led to rising expectations for what else analysis might do for her. Her initial reaction to discovering that she was no longer so inhibited was to crow with excitement and she set about testing her improvement as if to make up for lost time. After a few weeks, her reports about her expanding social life dwindled and in sessions her manner, which had become relaxed and spontaneous, became noticeably guarded again. Now, before going to the couch, she began each session with a long searching look at the analyst as if he had become a stranger. The analyst commented on the change in her behavior in ways that implied that the patient was resisting, even though he did not use that term. Still, it was clear that his intent in pointing out what she was doing wrong was to get her to stop it and get on with analyzing. This form of intervening proved counterproductive. The patient became increasingly sullen and uncooperative and while the sessions seemed barren to the analyst, who felt baffled by the turn of events, the patient missed no sessions and was unusually early in attending and unusually prompt in paying her bill.

Puzzled by this odd mixture of overcompliance and stubborn defiance, the analyst sought consultation. As he presented this picture, it became clear that he had not considered that the patient's behavior might be meaningful, even though her message was not couched in words. The consultant raised these questions: "Why did the patient look at him so searchingly? What might she be fearful about? Why was she so 'good' about attending, even coming early and why was she so prompt about paying her bill while at the same time withholding the cooperation in sessions that formerly came so easily to her?" Thinking about these Socratic questions, the analyst began to link the patient's odd behavior to the previous period of the analysis that had yielded such dramatic progress. He began to consider that the behavior he had lumped as resistive and hence unnecessary, even obstructive to the analysis, might be serving a useful purpose for the patient. Reviewing what he had learned about her history and dynamics, he then could construct a tentative case for why the patient *ought* to behave as she did. He could suppose that the patient, who had been so grateful for the diminution of her shyness and now wanted much more from him also felt guilty about her "greediness." He could also consider that his way of confronting her with her resistive behavior might well mean to her that he wanted her to stop holding back, get on with her treatment and make way for some sicker, more deserving patient. She should be content with half a loaf because she already had gotten more than she deserved. He entertained that his way of intervening could well have intensified her feelings of guilt. Armed with these new understandings, the analyst changed his approach to the patient. He first proposed that his way of pointing out how she was behaving, instead of helping her, had made her increasingly uncomfortable and, he gathered, also to feel much misunderstood. Her posture became more relaxed, though she offered little more than some grunts of assent. After a while, he added that it must have seemed that he thought she had no reason to act as she did and that he did not appreciate how distressed she was to be behaving so, and yet how impossible it felt to her to behave any differently. The patient then began to sniffle and then haltingly alluded to her feelings of guilt and the expectations she thought he had of her in a way that reassured the analyst that he finally was on the right track. He then relaxed and allowed the story to emerge in the patient's words and at her pace. She essentially confirmed the construction he had arrived at with the help of his consultant but added new historical material that helped to make sense of her foot dragging. She told about how as soon as she had learned to do anything for herself, to tie her shoelaces, for instance, mother never did them for her again. The inevitable price for achievement was abandonment, and she could hardly expect any different from the analyst. Opening up this behavior pattern and pattern of expectation permitted the patient to feel the abandonment she feared even while safely experiencing the analyst's presence. And she could then mourn the loss of support by her mother in both its real and fantasized aspects as well as appreciate that she would one day leave the analyst, rather than be left by him, and that too would be a sad as well as happy prospect (Schlesinger 1996).

MOURNING AND INTERPRETATION:
PRO AND CON

Mourning, like loving, is a natural, normal, human emotional state (Persons 1988, Kernberg 1974). Most analysts encounter loving in the context of the peculiar, defensive conditions that patients invent to detoxify what they regard as a potentially poisonous state. Analysts attempt to unravel the complications and distortions that are the familiar obstacles our neurotic patients put in the way of loving and being loved. As clinicians, we are concerned with distortions so severe that they may amount to the inability to love or to accept being loved.

It is much the same with mourning. We take for granted now that humans are born into relatedness and that loving and also hating are the glue that holds us together. When a relationship is threatened, when the premises of mutual attraction and settled attachment no longer are tenable, a more or less subtle process of detachment begins, and a train of emotional responses normally ensues. These include the familiar cognitive and emotional efforts to deal with the pain of actual or threatened separation occur (Kubler-Ross 1969).

Mourning is a natural, normal experience, a way of coming to terms with loss, and if it is to be successful, it should be experienced fully. A patient's reaction to loss might be excessive in amount, deviant in quality or both, and to that extent pathological. The clinician's first problem is diagnostic in these regards, to understand whether the patient's response to the loss is leading to normal mourning or toward defending against the pain of loss.

Loss, perhaps unacknowledged loss, is the major reason patients come to psychoanalysis. The experience of loss, however, is not the "problem." If there is a problem for analysis, it rather is in the way the patient avoids dealing with the experience of loss, in particular whether either the patient's immediate reaction to the awareness of loss or the patient's subsequent efforts interfere with the process of mourning.

These sequences of encounter, attachment, relationship, and then perhaps disillusionment, detachment, and separation occur in patients in analysis with perhaps even greater frequency than in the lives of non-analysands. After all, our patients are constantly having their emotional presuppositions challenged, and relationships both within the analytic cloister and outside are held up for examination and reexamination, experimentation, and refutation. There may be much to analyze in these goings on, but it does not include the simple fact that when relationships dissolve, the tension of impending separation is painful; significant relationships do not dissolve painlessly. These simple facts require witnessing by the analyst, recognition, clarification, and appreciation with empathy and patience, but not ever relentless interpreting. I overstate my argument here for sake of emphasis, of course, for I can think of no instance when relentless interpreting would be considered good analytic technique.

These reactions "belong"; they are "normal" and "healthy" and the analyst must be sensitive enough to recognize when the patient becomes intolerant of the pain. Then, rather than remaining fully engaged in mourning, the patient may attempt to "analyze" to defend against the painful experience of letting go. The analyst faces a delicate discrimination at these points, for the process of normal mourning, like working-through in general, is not continuous, but rather is episodic. Periods of deep involvement in mourning alternate with attention to other less serious matters and to lighter moods. The more obsessive patient may even worry that he is not sad enough and that the seriousness of his loss is being thrown into question by the moments of levity. For a commonplace illustration, recall the shifting moods at a wake when sorrow about loss and sadness that the departed is no longer with us alternates with the jokes one once shared with him and with sips of wine. Consider also the shifting moods at a college graduation when the joy of anticipation of a bright future alternates with tears at the loss of precious relationships and promises to stay in touch. The course of separation, like the course of true love is not smooth. In short, the analyst must be familiar with the normal, usually lumpy, processes both of becoming attached and of letting go in order to help the patient experience and appreciate the pains and pleasures that go with both. The analyst must reserve his more specific analytic efforts, that is interpretation, for the defensive impediments that patients erect to slow down the process, and those efforts too must be leavened by appreciating that sometimes it feels too painful to bear.

As in other areas, the analyst's main diagnostic problem is to figure out what the defense is *for*, not just what it is against. Another way of putting it is that the analyst should focus on what (perceived) problem of the patient is solved by this seeming pathological defending, not just on what it costs. The analyst should expect the patient to mourn whenever he experiences or anticipates loss; absence of mourning when it is called for should alert the analyst to consider the possible reasons.

The analyst must be able to discriminate among several possibilities, the "natural" rhythm of the mourning process, the temporary defensive interruptions when it hurts too much, and the more serious interruptions that represent a stubborn refusal to give up the lost object and a settling into chronic grieving rather than to permit mourning that would lead to the eventual surrender of the object. These diagnostic skills are not easy to learn, especially if the analyst has not yet suffered and worked through a significant loss in his own life.

REFERENCES

Kernberg, O. (1974). Barriers to falling and remaining in love. *Journal of the American Psychoanalytic Association* 22:486–511.

Kubler-Ross, E. (1969). *On Death and Dying.* New York: McMillan.

Mahler, M.S. (1972). On the first three subphases of the separation-individuation process. *International Journal of Psycho-Analysis* 53:333–338.

Person, E. (1988). *Dreams of Love and Fateful Encounters.* New York: Norton.

Pfeffer, A. (1993). After the analysis: analyst as both old and new object. *Journal of the American Psychoanalytic Association* 41: 323–337.

Schlesinger, H.J. (1995). The process of interpretation and the moment of change. *Journal of the American Psychoanalytic Association* 43:3 662–685.

———. (1996). The fear of being left half-cured. *Bulletin of the Menninger Clinic* 1996, 60:4, 428–448.

7

CHANGING HATEFUL FEELINGS BACK TO LOVING FEELINGS: THE WORK OF CHILD ANALYSIS

Discussion of Schlesinger's Chapter, "Technical Problems in Analyzing the Mourning Patient"

William Singletary, M.D.

I would like to begin with a quote from an 8-year-old boy who ranked this number one on his list of "feelings tips": "The tears of sadness put out the flames of anger, only to reveal the smoke of happiness." I think of this as a poetic rendering of Dr. Schlesinger's major thesis that phenomena associated with mourning are a central aspect of every analysis and need to be seen and appreciated for the patient to resolve conflicts, to develop, and to conclude a successful analysis.

DR. SCHLESINGER'S CONTRIBUTION

Let me briefly highlight Dr. Schlesinger's main points. First, Dr. Schlesinger stresses the ubiquity of mourning. The capacity to recognize and accept loss and to let it go is a necessary condition for maturation and development. A colleague told me about a 5-year-old boy who was crying at his birthday party, a usual occasion for happiness and celebration. When his mother asked why he was crying, he replied, "Because I'll never be 4 again." Dealing with loss is a daily experience. Next, Dr. Schlesinger mentions the necessity of coming to terms with limitations, with our finitude and with what we are not. This reminds me of what I feel is Dr. Mahler's (1988) most poignant description of the experience of the rapprochement child who has learned that he is not one with mother and that he is a small person in a big world:

> As a child first becomes aware of his status as a separate, helpless, and very small individual . . . there comes . . . a realization that he is very much dependent on his mother, that his mother is separate from him and that she and the father have their own interests and lives. The toddler realizes, in short, that he is by no means the center of the universe. This is the rapprochement crisis. (p. 149)

Dr. Schlesinger discusses three contexts in which the analyst can expect to deal with mourning. More than likely, the first context is the most familiar to you, that is, when the patient suffers the loss of a significant other. Less often appreciated, are reactions to loss of parts of the self, such as a sense of loss that patients may experience when parts of the self, such as chronic symptoms, change as a result of analysis. In such instances, both the indication that the patient is experiencing a sense of loss and the defenses against experiencing mourning may be quite subtle. Third, mourning is part of the response to therapeutic change, since every change involves loss as well as gain. For Dr. Schlesinger, unacknowledged loss is the major reason patients enter analysis. Thus, a central task of the analyst is to protect the mourning process by dealing with the patient's attempts to minimize pain by avoiding the experience of loss and the work of mourning. The analyst needs to help the patient become able to mourn fully. Central to Dr. Schlesinger's thinking is his model of the analytic process as a series of beginnings and endings, a succession of episodes in which the patient begins work on a particular issue that is then worked on and sufficiently resolved for the time being. With such resolution and achievement come a sense of ending or loss and a fear that continued resolution of conflict and further development will lead to the end of analysis and the loss of the analyst. As a defense against loss and mourning, the patient may attempt to deny, hide, or minimize such therapeutic change and achievement. Stalemates in analysis may be triggered by unacknowledged progress, and serious interruptions of the analytic process may represent a refusal to mourn and to give up the analyst.

True and lasting therapeutic change, with its associated mourning, does not come easily. When patients change and develop, I know that I'm in for trouble. Thanks to Dr. Schlesinger, I understand that when there's a sudden turbulence in a treatment that had seemed to be going well, the question to ask is not, "What's gone wrong?" but "What's gone right?" In other words, what significant positive development has occurred that has led the patient to experience an unacknowledged sense of loss, so that the current disruption represents a defense against mourning? Learning to expect regression and trouble at times of therapeutic change helps me, and the parents of the children whom I see, to keep a sense of where we are in the treatment process and to not be disheartened. This also helps me to better understand the patient's experience and to intervene effectively. Typically, this involves listening for and searching out the recent positive experience of the patient and, based on the patient's associations, interpreting the current symptoms as a reaction to this positive change.

PATHOLOGICAL INTERNAL STRUCTURE, REFUSAL TO MOURN, AND OBSTACLES TO CHANGE IN ANALYSIS[1]

In his conclusion, Dr. Schlesinger briefly mentions the obstacles patients may put in the way of loving and being loved. In his

---

[1]S. Kopp (1969) used the term "refusal to mourn" in his paper, "The Refusal to Mourn," as did M. Stark (1994) in her discussion of "relentless entitlement."

clinical material, he suggests a relationship between difficulties in mourning and difficulties in giving and receiving love, for example, the woman whose fear of bearing the pain of loss kept her defended against intimacy. However, he does not explicitly elaborate on such a connection. My sense is that one of our main tasks in analysis is to help patients develop the capacity to mourn so that they are able to love and be loved, to develop what Dr. Mahler referred to as libidinal object constancy, a sense of having a sustaining, loving, and comforting object inside. Difficulties with mourning seem to be intertwined with difficulties with object and self constancy.

In my clinical experience, there has been a certain group of challenging patients whose treatments most clearly reflect their great difficulty with the loss and mourning associated with therapeutic change. These patients (both children and adults) have great conflicts about receiving and giving love. However, as Dr. Schlesinger underscores, such patients have good reasons for these difficulties with love, change, and loss, reasons that need to be appreciated and understood. In fact, virtually all of these patients have experienced significant trauma such as deprivation, abuse, neglect, loss, or surgery early in life. Under such traumatic influences, an internalized world dominated by hostile self and object representations is established and then actively maintained. Hostile self and object constancy seems to me to be a useful way to conceptualize this type of pathological organization (Steiner 1993). Instead of disruptions in the therapeutic process that are precipitated by the analyst's empathic failures or by the patient's experiencing a lack of empathy and understanding (Wolf 1994), or by an inaccurate interpretation, positive experiences of self and other in the analytic setting are disruptive and seem to act as toxins or allergens (Singletary 2000).

In my work with such patients, I have found the concept of emotional diabetes to be clinically useful both in guiding my understanding and in talking to patients and parents. As diabetics are unable to utilize their available glucose, patients suffering from emotional diabetes (Matte-Blanco 1941, Kris 1976), while hungry and clamoring for love, are unable to utilize the love that they actually receive from the analyst, as well as from other significant people in their lives. In understanding such patients from a developmental point of view, considering them simply to lack libidinal self and object constancy does not seem sufficient. Concerns about the need to understand the relationship between the lack of object and self constancy and the remarkable stability of hostile internal objects as well as negative, hostile, and painful self-representations have been raised by a number of authors (Blum 1981 and 1996, Burland 1986, Kramer and Parens 1996, Parens 1972, Valenstein 1973, Weil 1985). Kramer and Akhtar (1988) defined object constancy as "the ability to retain a positive affective mental representation of the maternal object in her absence and when a child feels ambivalently toward her" (p. 554). The opposite state of affairs is an important aspect of the psychopathology under consideration here. The remarkable stability of negative, hostile representations of self and objects seems best conceptualized as hostile self and object constancy. With such patients, there is both a necessity and an *ability* to retain negative affective mental representations of self and object in spite of positive experiences. Dr. Mahler, toward the end of her career, saw the usefulness of the concept of a hostile object constancy that interferes with the utilization of what potentially good objects have to offer (Parens 2000). The patient's conflicts about giving and receiving love contribute to the active maintenance of hostile self and object representations and to a deficit of loving self and object images (Singletary 2000). An inability, or perhaps refusal, to mourn (Stark 1994, Kopp 1969) is an integral part of this pathology–maintaining process.

I have found the concept of an internal world of hostile self and objects linked by negative affects, which the patient *actively* seeks to maintain, to be a useful guide along the analytic journey and a helpful focus for clinical work. Unlike self psychology, which considers analysis as primarily a developmental process in which thwarted development is allowed to unfold (Mitchell 1988, Goldberg 1986), to me psychoanalysis seems best conceptualized as involving both therapeutic and developmental processes that are separate but complementary (Settlage 1992). Work with the patient's conflicts about giving and receiving love enables the patient to make use of the developmental aspects of the analytic situation. Developmental gains, in turn, modify and strengthen the patient's psychic structure, which contributes to an increased ability to work with unconscious conflicts (Settlage 1992).

Now, I would like to elaborate on Dr. Schlesinger's thoughts about mourning in response to effective interpretation. An effective interpretation is understood to cause a change or disruption in the patient's neurotic structure and the patient reacts to this change with what Dr. Schlesinger refers to as attempts at damage control, attempts to minimize the sense of instability and loss associated with change. Thus, the patient's response to an effective interpretation reflects both change and loss as well as resistance to change and loss. If the analyst consistently uses follow-up interpretations to prolong the state of change, instability, and loss, such change will eventually become structuralized (Schlesinger 1995).

I find Dr. Schlesinger's concept of the patient's attempts to control the damage inflicted by effective interpretation and change to be quite useful. Let me give a few brief clinical examples of what I consider to be some different, but related, methods of damage control that can be particularly disruptive. First, is biting the hand that feeds you and devaluing or trashing the analyst. Love is turned into hate, and the analyst is turned into a worthless piece of trash. The experience of a good analyst is turned into the experience of a bad analyst. This essentially kills off the internal representation of a good analyst and a good self, which are developing inside (Adler and Buie 1979). The recognition of goodness and love in one's self and others evokes envy in the internal hostile self and objects (Klein 1957, Lopez-Corvo 1995). For such patients gratitude is intolerable and they do not experience a heartfelt "thank you" (Klein 1957, McWilliams and Lependorf, 1990). In Japanese, the word for "thank you" also means "that which is easily lost" (Kitayama 1998). Thus, "thank you" or gratitude and transience are intimately connected (Kitayama 1998). Another 6-year-old boy, after having gotten a cup of water, tore up the cup saying, "You only got me water. You didn't get me food." We talked about this as his way to say, "thank you." In treatment, this leads to the negative therapeutic reaction (Etchegoyen 1999). The patient tries to undo any change that would destabilize his hostile internal world (Schlesinger 1995). An adult patient, at various times, talked about winning the lottery and tearing up the ticket, being let out of prison but refusing to leave, dying of thirst in the desert and finding an oasis, but leaving immediately, and in his words, of "hoping and praying that you (meaning me, the analyst) or my mother will take care of me. Then when you do, I say, 'Get the hell out of here!'" This same man, after a period of most significant analytic work and change, imagined the check which he was about to hand me to be a gun for killing me. Feelings of change and gratitude led him to want to destroy me. In a similar vein, a 10-year-old boy said to me, "I think I'm mean to you whenever I feel like I never want to leave you." For some patients, sadness and mourning feel intolerable, and "missing feelings" are to be avoided at all costs (Klein 1957, Zetzel 1965) For example, in the days immediately following his elaborate birthday party for Wrinkles, a raccoon puppet in my office, complete with a four-poster bed, which he and his family made along with a quilt, monogrammed pajamas, cupcakes with candles and hand-painted napkins, a 7-year-old boy began to kill, boil, grill, and eat this little raccoon, his most dear friend. He agreed when I said that if he killed and ate Wrinkles, that he could feel that he had him inside forever and would never lose him and have to be sad. Another young boy played with animal puppets and had one puppet protest that he did not want to get a good heart because then he would be able to feel sad. I think that these examples illustrate such patients' tremendous wishes for and the ways they fight against experiencing loving, helpful relationships that could be lost (Singletary 2000).

CLINICAL EXAMPLE: MOURNING AND THE PROCESS OF "CHANGING HATEFUL FEELINGS BACK INTO LOVING FEELINGS"

As an illustration of the usefulness of Dr. Schlesinger's thoughts about mourning in child analysis, I will briefly present some material from an analysis that ended a few years ago. I will focus on a period in the analysis when Bobby was making major changes and becoming better able to love and be loved, and his thoughts turned to loss and the eventual end of his analysis. I began seeing Bobby in analysis four times weekly right before his third birthday when his distraught parents consulted me immediately after discovering that Bobby was being neglected and emotionally abused by Rose, his sitter. Rose had taken care of Bobby five days a week for approximately ten hours a day since he was 12–18 months of age. When I first saw him, Bobby's difficulties included emotional distancing and withdrawal, as well as hostile, sadistic, and physically aggressive behavior. He had already developed a sadomasochistic way of relating; he seemed to enjoy taunting and hurting others and, on one occasion, he provocatively said to his father over and over, "kiss me, kick me." Early in analysis I was faced with the challenge of helping Bobby become emotionally engaged. In addition to talking about how he did things by himself, I intruded, as gently and as playfully as possible, into his solitary and affectless play. At first, I included Bobby's parents in our sessions in order to help them understand Bobby's difficulties and how to actively engage him. After six months of treatment, during a session, Bobby and his mother sang and then made a tape recording of a song that he had recently learned, "There's a Little Wheel Turning in My Heart," and later Bobby made a paper heart with a wheel in it, which would turn.

Dr. Schlesinger's ideas helped in understanding Bobby's paradoxical reaction to opening his heart to loving and being loved. Particularly after warm and loving times with his parents, Bobby would become out of control and seem to enjoy hitting, kicking, and spitting. These reactions were also a definite part of our work, for example, after a pleasurable time with an increased sense of warmth and closeness between us, Bobby bit a hole in my couch. In response to feeling loved and loving, Bobby felt small and vulnerable, and his angry, destructive attack gave him a sense of power and control over the needed and loved person whom he was afraid he would lose. On one of these occasions I said, "Bobby, I think that whenever you're mean to people, it's because you're feeling more loving and caring." Bobby grinned and said, "I'll pay you a quarter for that." We also talked about how instead of having missing feelings for people, like when I went away on vacation or when his mommy put him to bed at night, or even just between our sessions, he would be angry at us. Instead of missing us and feeling sad, he would be angry, turn us into bad and mean people in his head and heart, kill us off as good people inside of him, and then feel all alone. Helping his parents set limits and punish Bobby in helpful ways and finding ways for Bobby to make reparation for his attacks, for example cleaning the wall in my office after he angrily marked on it, were important aspects of our work. Bobby needed to develop a helpful conscience and to be able to consciously experience guilt for his trashing of whatever and whomever he considered to be good and valuable. At the beginning of the fourth year of Bobby's analysis, Bobby and I talked about his needing to keep me with him in his heart in the evenings when he typically had more behavior problems. Also, I asked his mother to help Bobby protect the things that he made with me and took home with him to help him with his self-control, but that were usually lost or destroyed. One day Bobby again recorded the song, "There's a Little Wheel Turning in My Heart." Then he made a drawing of me with a bomb nearby, that was set to go off in sixty seconds. Bobby raced against the clock and managed to put tape around his drawing of me and thereby protected me from the explosion. Bobby was playing about his internal struggle between his loving feelings and his hating feelings and was protecting his image of me as a loved and loving person from his destructive attacks. In our sessions, Bobby began to make tapes of love songs and of children's stories and fairytales. He said the story of Cinderella was like our work because it was about loving feelings changing to hating feelings and then changing back to loving feelings. Cinderella had loving parents who died, then she had a mean stepmother, and then she had a loving prince.

Next, Bobby made a Love Book. On one page Bobby proclaimed:

> In order to make your love feelings work the best in the world, even if it's the worst thing in your whole life, is you have to say to your mom, Mom I'm getting angry!!! so that she can stop you and so that you can stop yourself, then you'll have the best life in the whole wide world.

On another page, Bobby said:

> The vampire, which is a bad guy, plus the sun, which is a good guy, equals the vampire turning into a pile of dust and the sun still existing.

Clearly, Bobby was making major changes in his internal world; love was winning out over hate. He was developing a loving self and object constancy and, along with this, a greater capacity for mentalization, for thinking and talking about his feelings, and for self-control.

In a session immediately after we finished his Love Book, what happened between Bobby and me led me to think about Dr. Schlesinger's work. Uncharacteristically, Bobby was not sure what to do but said, "After we think of what to do, we can start taping our sessions." Let me spell out why I thought of Dr.

Schlesinger right at this point. After a period of significant change and development, there was a loss of focus in our work and an interest in doing something, taping the sessions, which would keep us together forever. This alerted me to the possibility that Bobby was attempting to avoid a sense of loss occasioned by his recent development. I wondered aloud about why he would want to tape the sessions and Bobby replied, "because someday I won't be coming here, and I might forget something if I don't have the tapes."

When I suggested that we make a book instead, Bobby became very excited and said, "What we could write are important things like, this one day I started to be able to work on my feelings a lot better. I'm better at stopping myself and mommy's helping me stop myself. Two people working to help one person can kill one bad guy (inside) every day." I said, "You're really getting better so that you think about someday you won't need to come here anymore." Bobby agreed and looked sad. Bobby talked about feeling sad about something that it was good to feel sad about. Then we started Bobby's Memory-Love Book. The first entry reads:

> This book gets started at the end of about 600 sessions. My love feelings started getting better and better. I started being able to work on my feelings much better.
>
> I am feeling sad about someday I will stop doing my sessions and sessions are really important to me. I want to be able to remember all of my sessions.

After that Bobby and I played countless battles in which love defeated hate and made numerous hearts in which loving feelings and hating feelings get together and make sad feelings. Love feelings that also contain sadness and hate are, according to Bobby, the best kind of love feelings in the whole world.

Let me close with another entry from Bobby's Memory-Love Book:

Today in the morning I wanted waffles for breakfast. It was a school morning so I couldn't. I asked mom to cuddle with me, so she did. And then I said to her, 'Mommy, I love you.' Even though I was mad, I was really sad and the sad feelings were there instead of the mad feelings and the hate feelings. And I loved you even though the sad feelings were there. I had love feelings and sad feelings.

I think we can see how much it helped Bobby to become able to feel sad and to mourn the loss of his fantasy of being one person with an all-good and all-powerful mother who would give him whatever he wanted. Instead of hating and attacking his less than perfect mother, he could feel sad and mourn and accept his own and his mother's limitations. In doing this, he could have a good-enough mother who would always be in his heart, whom he could love and who could love, protect, comfort, and sustain him.

REFERENCES

Adler, G. and Buie, D. (1979). Aloneness and borderline psychopathology: possible relevance of child development issues. *International Journal of Psycho-Analysis* 60: 83–96.

Blum, H. (1981). Object inconstancy and paranoid conspiracy. *Journal of the American Psychoanalytic Association* 29: 789–813.

————. (1996). Perspectives on internalization, consolidation, and change: concluding reflections. In *The Internal Mother: Conceptual and Technical Aspects of Object Constancy*, ed. S. Akhtar, S. Kramer, and H. Parens, pp. 173–201. Northvale, NJ: Jason Aronson Inc.

Burland, J. A. (1986). The vicissitudes of maternal deprivation. In *Self and Object Constancy: Clinical and Theoretical Perspectives*, ed. R. Lax, S. Bach, and J. A. Burland, pp. 224–347. New York: Guilford Press.

Etchegoyen, R.H. (1999). *The Fundamentals of Psychoanalytic Technique*. London: Karnac Books.

Goldberg, A. (1986). Reply. *Contemporary Psychoanalysis* 22: 387–388.

Hughes, D. (1997). *Facilitating Developmental Attachment: The Road to Emotional Recovery and Behavioral Change in Foster and Adopted Children*. Northvale, NJ: Jason Aronson Inc.

Kitayama, O. (1998). Transience: its beauty and danger. *International Journal of Psycho-Analysis* 79: 937–942.

Klein, M. (1957). "Envy and Gratitude." In *The Writings of Melanie Klein, Vol. 3, Envy and Gratitude and Other Works, 1946–1963*. New York: The Free Press. 1984.

Kopp, S. (1969). The refusal to mourn. *Voices* 46: 30–35.

Kramer, S. and Akhtar, S. (1988). The developmental context of internalized preoudipal object relations—clinical applications of Mahler's theory of symbiosis and separation-individuation. *Psychoanalytic Quarterly* 57: 547–576.

Kramer, S. and Parens, H. (1996). Multiple perspectives on object constancy. In *The Internal Mother: Conceptual and Technical Aspects of Object Constancy*. ed. S. Akhtar, S. Kramer, and H. Parens, pp. 1–14. Northvale, NJ: Jason Aronson Inc.

Kris, A. (1976). On wanting too much: the "exceptions" revisited. *International Journal of Psycho-Analysis* 57: 85–95.

Lopez-Corvo, R. (1995). *Self-Envy: Therapy in the Divided Internal World*. Northvale, NJ: Jason Aronson Inc.

Mahler, M.S. (1988). *The Memoirs of Margaret S. Mahler*, ed. P. Stepansky. New York: The Free Press.

Matte-Blanco, I. (1941). On introjection and the process of psychic metabolism. *International Journal of Psycho-Analysis* 22: 17–36.

McWilliams, M. and Lependorf, S. (1990). Narcissistic pathology of every day life: the denial of remorse and gratitude. *Contemporary Psychoanalysis* 26: 430–451.

Mitchell, S. (1988). *Relational Concepts in Psychoanalysis: An Integration*. Cambridge, MA: Harvard University Press.

Parens, H. (1972). Book review: Rudolph Ekstein's *The Challenge: Despair and Hope in the Conquest of Inner Space*. *Psychoanalytic Quarterly* 41: 616–623.

———. (2000). Personal communication.

Schlesinger, H. (1995). The process of interpretation and the moment of change. *Journal of the American Psychoanalytic Association* 43: 663–688.

Settlage, C.F. (1992). Psychoanalytic observations on adult development in life and in the therapeutic relationship. *Psychoanalysis and Contemporary Thought* 15: 349–374.

Singletary, W. (2000). *Emotional diabetes: a syndrome of hostile self and object constancy*. Presented at the Meetings of The American Psychoanalytic Association vulnerable child workshop. Chicago, IL, May.

Stark, M. (1994). *Working with Resistance*. Northvale, NJ: Jason Aronson Inc.

Steiner, J. (1993). *Psychic Retreats: Pathological Organizations in Psychotic, Neurotic, and Borderline Patients.* London: Routledge.

Valenstein, A. (1973). On attachment to painful feelings and the negative therapeutic reaction. *Psychoanalytic Study of the Child* 28: 365–392.

Weil, A.P. (1985). Thoughts about early pathology. *Journal of the American Psychoanalytic Association* 33: 335–352.

Wolf, E. (1994). Self-object experiences: developments, psychopathology, treatment. In *Mahler and Kohut: Perspectives on Development, Psychopathology, and Technique*, ed. S. Kramer and S. Akhtar, pp. 65–96. Northvale, NJ: Jason Aronson Inc.

Zetzel, E. (1965). On the incapacity to bear depression. In *The Capacity for Emotional Growth*, E. Zetzel, pp. 82–114. New York: International Universities Press. 1970.

8

AN OBSTACLE TO THE CHILD'S COPING WITH OBJECT LOSS

Henri Parens, M.D.

In this chapter, I want to revisit the question we have considered for decades: Can the child actually mourn the loss of a libidinal object? Some (Wolfenstein 1966, 1974, Nagera 1970) have doubts that a child can do so; others (R. Furman 1964, 1973, E. Furman 1974, H. Hardin and D. Hardin 2000) think otherwise. My clinical and observational experience leads me to share the view that given requisite conditions, a child can mourn such a loss. And I want to focus here on one of the requisite conditions which, when it does not exist, seems to impede many a child's efforts to mourn and thereby implement his potential ability to cope with actual libidinal object loss. What I focus on has also been observed by others, especially by Robert Furman and Erna Furman, whose work on childhood loss is clinically and theoretically seminal and has duly attained the status of basic reference on this question. The obstacle I want to address is the commonly found resistance in the adults in a given child's world to helping the child bear his or her enormously painful reactions to the loss a highly emotionally invested object and to sustain the child's efforts to cope with that loss.

In an effort to clarify the challenge to the child of the experience of libidinal object loss, consider the line of thought that the objects available to help the child are in essence the child's "auxiliary egos" (Spitz[1] 1965). I use the concept "auxiliary ego" rather than "object" here to highlight the key role the emotionally invested adult plays in helping the child cope with highly taxing adaptation challenges; few are more taxing than the challenge of libidinal object loss. That is, in development, we view such objects as auxiliaries to the child's ego. Where the child's ego functions are not equal to a coping task, it commonly falls to the emotionally invested adult to act on behalf of the child's coping functions, thus as an "auxiliary ego." Sorting out the child's average-expectable operative auxiliary egos, I call attention to three categories: (1) the mental health professional auxiliary ego, namely ourselves; (2) the educational child helper, for example, a teacher or daycare worker; and (3) and most critical, the remaining parent or his or her substitute. I will only touch on the first two, and more extensively detail our gratifying experience in helping a mother help her two young children mourn the loss of their father.

In preparation for a presentation that occurred at the 5th Annual Margaret S. Mahler Symposium (1974) which addressed the issue of object loss in childhood and its effects on separation-individuation, our child analysis study group reviewed the video-tape to be presented by our esteemed colleague Humberto Nagera

---

[1]Twenty years before, in 1946, in his introducing us to *anaclitic depression,* Spitz observed that young children can be helped to tolerate the loss by providing the child with a substitutive libidinal object. Time does not permit an exploration here of the bearing that Spitz said may have on the issue I address in this article. There are significant differences between anaclitic depression and mourning, the developmental timetable of object relatedness being a key differential parameter, but they do have a common critical precipitant, libidinal object loss.

(1970). The aim of Nagera's 1974 presentation was to illustrate how difficult it is for young children to acknowledge and deal with the death of a parent. The video showed the nursery school activities of a 3-year-old whose mother had just died of cancer. Our group closely viewed the video several times because we were struck by unexpected findings. First is that we found five or six instances where the child made some reference to hospitals, to illness, and to her mother. Second and somewhat surprising, we found that in each instance, the well-meaning nursery school teacher redirected the child's preoccupation, asking her to focus instead on the activity going on at the time. This, we thought might occur in a "regular" nursery school. But this occurred in a nursery that is part of a psychiatric clinic and research center. My comment is not intended as a criticism. It aims to emphasize what we learned from it, the conclusion to which it brought us. It is that many adults find it painfully difficult to tolerate a young child's experiencing intense psychic pain. And, as no doubt others have found, we were made aware of the fact that helping such a child deal with his/her feelings, thoughts, and fantasies is extremely painful not only for the remaining parent, but is also very taxing for every therapist, and is equally difficult for teachers. Yet, we know that we cannot help a child cope with painful experiences without empathetically allowing the child's affects to resonate within our own psyche, with our own experiences of object loss, an experience unavoidably painful to a greater or lesser degree for each of us. Such empathy is unavoidably painful for two reasons. First, many of us are notably pained to see and let ourselves resonate with young children's emotional suffering. And second, because, as Schlesinger said at this Mahler Symposium, none of us can completely resolve the loss of our own libidinal objects, given that early-life libidinal cathexes are indelible (Freud 1939), and therefore remain within our psyches even well after mourning fades. This latter factor is reflective of Jacobson's (1964) and Mahler's (Mahler, Pine, and Bergman 1975) view that we all retain yearnings for reunion with the mother of symbiosis. And Zetzel's (1965)

admonition to us that we all must learn to tolerate depression, that
it is consistent with normal development, strikes directly to the
point I am addressing.

The degree to which many adults cannot help children mourn
probably bears on these adults' not being able to tolerate well
enough their own traumatizing inner and outer life experiences.
And it is further complicated by the still strongly held erroneous
view that children are too young to experience, to suffer, to
understand, or to internalize traumatic events to which they are
exposed. For example, 5-year-old Rose several times walked into
kindergarten and exclaimed dramatically "Oh, I had such a terrible
bus ride!" To this her well-meaning and quite sophisticated young
teacher would reply "Rose, we'll like you even if your bus ride
was very pleasant," feeling, as she told Rose's mother, that Rose
was asking for attention. The teacher seemed not to hear the child's
inner pressure and efforts to tell her that by the age of 5 she had
already had two traumatic ear surgical procedures, had witnessed
a hemmorrhagic catastrophe occur to her mother, had been painfully dropped by a disturbed relative before she died of cancer, and
for some time now her mother and father were constantly arguing
and threatening separation. What made this teacher unable to hear
Rose's affective and anxiety-ridden appeal for help? That's not all.
Rose was seen for one year in psychotherapy by a clinician whose
major efforts, according to Rose's parents, were aimed at trying
to get the child to pull herself together and admonished the parents
to set firm limits with her progressively intensifying self-destructive acts including getting her hand burned and opening the car
door while mother was driving it 50 miles per hour. What pre-
vented this quite experienced, capable, and responsible clinician
from prescribing in my opinion a better course of therapy for this
anxiety-ridden child? Is there a general tendency in adults, including ourselves perhaps more than we think, to encourage children
to deny and repress affects and perceived reality events, to their
detriment?

The domain of libidinal object loss is very wide. Let me

narrow our focus to object loss through death. It is established now in all mental health subdisciplines that no object loss has the finiteness and taxes the self as does libidinal object loss through death. Furthermore, it has a variable impact on the child, depending on the suddenness or protractedness of the loss event, on the stage of development of the id, ego, and superego, on the quality of preexisting, current, and subsequent object relations—that to the lost object, the surviving parent, and siblings, or parent substitutes. And, as the Furmans report in their work, the experience we as clinicians, as transference objects, and especially as auxiliary egos, or our teachers, bring to the child subjected to loss will also play its part in how that child experiences that loss. But most of all, none is more influential in the child's efforts to cope with that loss than the remaining parent is.

I would like to detail some of the steps we took in helping a mother help her two children cope with the death of their father. Let me first say a few words on methods of helping parents help their children, then present with some detail that of his sister Temmy who was then almost 6½, and I would like to close with a few remarks on the specific steps we took to help the mother help her two children.

HELPING PARENTS WITH THE DIFFICULTIES OF BEING PARENTS

Helping parents with the myriad tasks that come with being parents is long established in mental health. Here I will touch only on a limited number of efforts made by psychodynamically informed clinicians and theorists. I do so well aware that a number of other interdigitating disciplines are equally committed and productive in their efforts to achieve these goals, for instance, the attachment school, developmental and behavioral psychology, and so on. As psychodynamic child psychiatry emerged and established itself this century, social workers who for decades used

the Eastern Pennsylvania Psychiatric Institute (Philadelphia). The mothers brought all their children who were not in school, but it was those children whom we saw since birth who were our primary research subjects. The mothers cared for their infants; the project staff observed and at given moments intervened education-ally. The preschool children were free to move from the Infant Area, where their mothers tended to stay, to and from an adjacent Toddler Area, which was equipped to meet toddlers' needs. Our contract with these mothers simply stated that if they permitted us to observe naturalistically the development of their children, we would attempt to the best of our ability to answer any questions they had about the meaning of their children's behavior and their rearing. (For greater detail of the project population, observation and intervention methods, and the research strategy implemented see Parens 1979, Chapter 4.)

In this setting we saw Mrs. Z from the time when Temmy was 17 weeks of age and we saw Bernie from the time of his birth. Mrs. Z's oldest son, whom we did not see in the project, was ten years older than Temmy, and Temmy in turn was 22 months older than Bernie.

The Case of Bernie

Bernie was an active, robust neonate who matured and developed well during his first year. Mother–child relation developed with good mutuality. Drives and ego development, symbiosis and entry into separation-individualization proceeded quite well, despite Bernie's being subjected to a Denny-Brown splint twenty-four hours a day from age 3 to 9 months and part of the day thereafter until he was about 1 year old. His immobilized feet limited motility in consequence of which, I believe, some difficulties in age-adequately mediating hostile destructiveness emerged early, causing moderate difficulties between mother and child from about 12 months of age on. In addition to this factor, because of

long-existing internal conflicts over her own aggression, at
Mrs. Z had much difficulty in setting limits reasonably with
very active son. Progressively Bernie expressed distress at his mother
quiet but threatening way of not allowing him to do things
strivings for autonomy were compelling him into. At 18 months,
he would look at something he wanted to take hold of or touch
and would clasp one hand with the other, as if to hold it from
touching a prohibited object. This motorically expressed inhibition
manifested for perhaps six months. During his second year, Bernie
gradually accommodated to mother's demands for self-control and
the hand clasping decreased, but his mood and relations became
intermittently morose. Mrs. Z and Bernie were mutually capable
of affectionate interaction, play, and there was much quieting now
in their former battle of wills. Bernie progressively became able
to express disappointment and anger quite reasonably with her. All
in all, dominantly their relationship was good and stable. As to
father, his sister Temmy, and adolescent brother, available evidence
indicated good relatedness, with identification especially with father.
Toilet training proceeded rather unobtrusively, with no apparent
difficulty.

   With entry into his third year of life, from about 26 months,
Bernie's affectionate interaction with mother became erotic and
spread to a project staff woman whom he engaged in much fantasy
play. By contrast, with several males in our project his attitude
became more overtly morose and persistently hostile and phallic
aggressive. At less than 3, he would greet me occasionally with a
raised fist as if to say "You want this!" In part, I ascribed this
hostility toward me to my efforts to help his mother set limits more
reasonably, with less threat and hostility toward Bernie. In consequence it may be that I came to serve as the advocate of limit-
setting and he displaced onto me, although I was not the only male
he came to experience negatively, the hostility that was aroused
by his mother's limit-setting as well as his mother's own significant
conflict-bound aggression. How much this emotional investment
of hostility might have come from his relationship to his father

was also experienced toward his father, I was not able to
certain. With his older brother and sister he acted at times angrily,
times affectionately.

From about 2½, we saw much evidence of Bernie's castration
complex. With our aforementioned staff woman he enacted a
strikingly lucid impregnation fantasy. As this woman sat on the
floor engaged in play with him, he picked up a plastic spoon and
a pistol, pretended to shoot something into the spoon, put down
the pistol, gently and with care just slightly lifted the tip of the
woman's skirt and proceeded to put the spoon under her skirt.
Fascinated by this play, the staff woman allowed its development,
but at this point she adroitly moved and withdrew from this
contact. Fantasies of pregnancy and of sexual play dominated.

Castration anxiety mounted as his oedipal wishes proliferated
in fantasy play. At about 2 years and 8 months, he began to have
asthmatic episodes. We also noted an upsurge of hostility in him
toward people in general, although he continued to also experience reliable warmth and closeness with his mother and sister. This
hostility did not spare even himself: now he would slap his head
when he transgressed.

Just a few days under 3 years of age he broke a wooden spoon
his mother had used to tap his hands lightly when he touched
things he was told not to touch. We learned that mother had used
this spoon for a long time and wondered if his past hand-clasping
came from this source. I want to emphasize that Mrs. Z's ambivalence and marked anxiety about her own hostility, rather than
brutality, is what Bernie lived with. Several days later after breaking
the wooden spoon, Bernie experienced an acute hysterical paralysis of both legs: crawling he said pitifully to his mother, "Can't
walk."

When they came to the project the next day, mother carried
him in; he was acutely anxious. In keeping with our contract with
the mothers we responded to Mrs. Z's distressed asking for an
explanation of what was going on in Bernie. Our custom was to
answer questions when asked, children having the option to hear

what we say. In fact we articulated answers so that child and mother might understand. Mrs. Z told us that Bernie visited the doctor's the day before. He had gotten two booster shots, grabbed his penis when he got the shots, and checked repeatedly mother said, "Like to see if his penis is still there." By way of describing what happens to many a boy around the age of 3, I talked about their experiencing castration anxiety, reiterating it in varying ways to facilitate its being heard. Bernie's anxiety gradually softened as I spoke to the mothers and children in the room. Gradually within 45 minutes, with the assistance of Dr. B, another staff psychiatrist–psychoanalyst with whom Bernie had recently been selectively interacting, Bernie moved slowly and progressively and was able to walk down the hall for snacks (Parens and Pollock 1981). The removal of his paralysis by our carefully worded explanation of his castration anxiety and Oedipus complex was not novel to these mothers and children.

In the year that followed, Bernie's vigorous entry into the Oedipus complex quieted some. Influenced especially by his heightened castration anxiety and our ability to help him resolve the hysterical paralysis he suffered, his relation to staff men warmed significantly.

When Bernie was just past 3 his father sustained a lethal work-related injury that afflicted vital body organs, and he was hospitalized for nearly ten months. It became necessary then for mother to work outside the home. Early during this time Bernie, Temmy, and mother all seemed subdued during the occasional observational sessions they attended. Gradually their worries became less pressing as they adapted to father's hospitalization. When father returned home he was terribly debilitated. When Bernie was 4 years and 3 months of age, father's condition worsened and he again entered the hospital. Coincidentally at this time Mrs. Z lost her outside job and became overtly depressed. In one session, Bernie was lying on the couch, his head on mother's lap. He rejected a number of peer invitations to come and play, until his friend Harold coaxed him successfully. He then mobilized and, pistol in hand joined his friend Harold in play. Gradually over the weeks that passed his mood lightened, he played well with the staff women, and his relation to the men continued to progressively become friendlier. Father remained in the hospital, his condition worsening. At about this time, Temmy's spelling the word *die* with a staff woman (E.H.) led us to talking about children's feelings when father becomes terribly ill, is in the hospital for a long time, and everyone, including the children fear he may die.

More and more then we saw Bernie's developing a game with his good friend Harold. He would then provoke Harold to chase him. Squealing with anxious excitement, he allowed Harold to catch him. Then they would wrestle; Bernie's activity seemed only self-protective and suggested that he could not even benignly aggress against Harold as Harold could so reasonably against him. At some point when Harold became increasingly intense, Bernie would anxiously plead "Get him off me." He might even become tearful, very much to Harold's dismay. Bernie might then slap himself on the head several times. He would finally return to his mother, sad and anxious.

In research conference staff questioned if the prime defensive operation in this passive–aggressive activity resulted from the inhibition of hostile destructive feelings toward his ambivalently emotionally invested father, who was then most likely experienced as the object of his Oedipal rivalry as well as the loved father who was frighteningly ill. Conflicted by these feelings, which were layered on top of past accumulations of hostility experienced in his relationship with his mother, Bernie displaced and acted these out with his good friend Harold. Empathically, some of us felt that Bernie's defensive passivity was too great. Associated with this, in addition to his seeming erotic passivity enacted with Harold, we had seen Bernie's stuffing toys in his pockets making them bulge and once he filled his shirt with toys so that he looked pregnant. The sequence of these observable behaviors and the dynamic inferences we made of them led some of us to feel that psychotherapy was warranted and it was undertaken by Dr. B.

During the ensuing months, the relationship between Bernie and Harold consolidated further. Bernie now said, in the observation setting, to Dr. B that his father had lost a lot of weight, he hadn't seen him for four months, and *that he may die.*[2] Several days later, as not unusual he was play fighting with Harold. After several minutes with his fist he lightly hit Harold on the head. Immediately terrified, he said "Sorry." Harold re-engaged in wrestling and Bernie made no move at all to fight back. As part of our interventional research strategy, I elected to describe what I saw and audibly, so that Bernie could hear me, I said to his mother that Bernie seems terribly afraid that if he fights back he will hurt his friend Harold very badly. There was no change in his wrestling. I added to his mother that often when a boy's father is very sick, the boy thinks that somehow it is his fault. I went on, you know how boys get jealous of their daddies even though they love him very much. Bernie's wrestling immediately became more reasonably assertive and aggressive.

When Bernie was 4½ years old, his father died. We saw Bernie one week later. I had never seen Bernie so sad, soft, and cuddly when he played with a senior staff woman. Mrs. Z was depressed, speechless with our staff women to whom she spoke from time to time. Three days later Bernie was despondent on his mother's lap. Since father died, mother said softly, Bernie has been very upset and wetting the bed. Mrs. Z said that Bernie talks about his father's having died (but that Temmy does not). As we went on, Bernie still on his mother's lap, listening, we talked about how angry we become when a person we love gets sick, and then when that person dies, we feel even angrier. Then, because we have been angry with Daddy, sometimes a child feels that his anger is what made Daddy sick and die. Of course that's not true. And we need

---

[2]Though a 4-year-old has some ideas of what "to die" means, we have much evidence to show that he does not cognitively grasp the finality of dying, that it is not reversible. At this age, an object may die but be alive again the next moment.

to explain, even many times, and be sure that children understand what really made Daddy so sick, and lose so much weight, and even die. Being angry with Daddy is not what makes a Daddy become sick and die.

The next session, Mother and Bernie, Temmy somewhat less so, appeared now predictably low-keyed if not outright sad. Mrs. Z said that she didn't understand some of things Bernie was saying, that they made no sense. She didn't know how to handle that. For instance, she said that Bernie had said to her that maybe they could take Daddy out of the ground, bring him to the hospital, and Dr. Parens could make him better. What could she say to that? She knew that it would not be helpful to say that Bernie was being silly and she just didn't know what to say or do. I pointed out that in the child's mind the limits of what is and is not possible are not yet well established, that although Bernie's thought seems quite unreasonable, it is not. It is a wish, a fantasy of hope. And the way to address it with the child, I feel, is to take the child's question seriously, to just be upfront with the child, and in the context of feeling sadness and pain to explain what is possible and what is not. I emphasized that it is important to allow the child not only to feel sad and comfort the child as best as Mom can, but to also allow the child to say whatever the child thinks and feels and to address it as truthfully as one can. We took occasion to reiterate this many times with regard to dealing with a child's feelings of loss, of sadness, of anger, and so on as occasions presented themselves.

I want to interrupt my narrative to point out that the reason I am presenting Bernie's development in some detail is to highlight his vulnerability during the period when his father was nearing death and died. My aim is to show that a mother can be helped to be more effectively helpful to her child even when the child is young and so vulnerable.

Four days later Mrs. Z and Bernie came into the Project Area, Bernie hiding behind his mother, glued to her. He stayed with us in the Infant Area, his coat over his head, his face protected from view. Mrs. Z said he asked to come. One mother—the mothers had become a fairly cohesive, mutually supportive and friendly group and they would often try to intervene with others' children in helpful ways—brought up, as if to inform Bernie, that Harold was not here today because he has the mumps. I elected to say that I would not be surprised if Bernie thought that somehow, maybe Harold got the mumps because Bernie hit him when they were wrestling. It is important, I went on, to talk with children about such things, to explain that two friends fighting does not cause one of them to get the mumps, but that mumps is caused by a bug like the one that causes a cold. His coat removed, Bernie's face now visible was glum and morose. Gradually he moved into nonspecific fantasy play with Dr. B. When his sister came in at this time, he related to her placidly but well and soon was off, pistol in hand, to the Toddler Area.

Two weeks later, for two days Bernie had been pressured, hyperactive. In wrestling with Harold, Bernie inadvertently it seemed stepped on Harold's index finger. Harold cried out softly. Bernie became immediately upset, went to his mother, despondent, and asked that she hold him. I said to the mothers, how Bernie might again, with this little accident, feel that if he lets himself go reasonably, be reasonably active and wrestle, he fears he might hurt people he likes, or even destroy them. His mother said something to him softly. Mrs. Z then said that Bernie told his sister that "Daddy died because I was bad." By this time in our work with them we could tell these mothers that being angry with father may at times lead a child to wish father would get hurt, or not come back home, or even die. That in the best of father and child relationships, being angry with father is unavoidable, that young children often have hurtful wishes like that, including that father would die, but that their notion of being dead is that it is not the end, that death is not finite.

Nearly four months after father's death at home, he tells his mother from time to time that he is feeling sad that Daddy is not here. Both mother and Bernie do look sad at times alternately, at times simultaneously. Let me just mention that in his therapy sessions with Dr. B., Bernie was also able to talk about his father's death, and to play at crashes, accidents, and attach them to father's death. Now we began to see more phallic aggression return, with boxing and carrying a gun. His mood was good. At home, mother told us he was looking at girls in a magazine. Mother grinned and said that when she asked him which one he would like to marry, he surprised her a bit by saying "you." Now we saw waxing and waning of his reemerging aggression along with sexuality, oedipal complex, and conflict behaviors (Parens, Pollock, Stern, and Kramer 1976), as it seemed influenced by the status of his sadness and working on the loss of father.

Five months after his father's death, there was a resurgence of Bernie's castration anxiety, overreacting to a fall from a chair. Quite histrionic, he complained he had hurt his thigh and feeling it opportune, I said that it really had made me think of when Bernie went to the doctor's, got a shot in his thigh, and worried terribly that maybe the doctor had damaged his penis. His mood lifted immediately and he returned to a good level of busy-ness.

At this time, he was working on separating from his therapist, who was leaving our clinic. Bernie was able to cry and seemed not to be overly angry. His mother was readily available to him and responsive to his talking about his therapist's leaving. His attention at this time turned especially to a girl peer in the neighborhood, an overtly sexualized relatedness. Nonetheless he developed some wheezing and for the first time since before father's death, Mrs. Z put him back on asthma medication.

When Bernie was 5 years and 4 months, he began to show signs of what eventuated into a most dramatic falling in love with one of our social work students who participated in early childhood observations. The affect, the dialogues with mother pertaining to his yearning, wishes, and plans to get her to come to his home, his loving looks, phallic exhibitionistic preening, were evidence of love feeling of large proportion.

Bernie's mother was appreciative of our discussion, which she repeatedly initiated, most now carried out while Bernie was in the Toddler Area, a good distance from hearing us. She too was able to respect her son's deep yearning, the genuineness of his love feelings, and to not ridicule or depreciate his experience. As a result she was not only rewarded by his communication with her, she was also able to help him increase his reality testing, to help him tolerate one after another disappointment, and even more to make it a positive experience.

When he was about 5 years and 10 months, time came for our social work student to tell Bernie that in three weeks she would be leaving our Institute. I will conclude this observational material with the dramatic weekend that followed Bernie's being told by Miss L that she would be leaving. On the Friday, after our project session Bernie visited Harold. He was fine, Harold's mother told us. She did notice that whereas Bernie affectionately had called Harold's father "Uncle Ned," this afternoon he called him "Dad" and "Pop." That Sunday, Mrs. Z, Bernie, and Temmy went to church, as was their custom. Several hours later, Bernie acutely looked more and more ill. He developed a marked asthmatic attack, the first one in over a year, and had to be taken to the emergency room. The following Tuesday, at our next meeting, Mrs. Z related the events of the weekend. She realized with understanding that Bernie's having called Harold's father "Dad," his learning that he would soon have to separate from Miss L, were intensified by and had to do with the fact that the church services to which Bernie and his family went on Sunday was the one where Bernie's father's funeral services had been held (which Bernie had attended.) Bernie was with us when the mothers and staff talked about the very real pain we all feel when we lose someone we love. Mrs. Z told us that wheezing, while sitting in the living room chair father used to habitually occupy, Bernie had said, "I wish Daddy was here and I was in the ground." Despite her pain, Mrs. Z told Bernie she was certain that Daddy would not want that. She was crying softly and Bernie showed the facial evidence of deeply felt sadness and pain. Bernie's asthmatic reactivity lasted several days.

Two weeks later, his parting with Miss L was very moving. He was helped in his work of separation by Harold's younger sister, who had had her eye on him for some time now. Nonetheless, he, his mother, and sister continued to openly refer to Daddy. Mrs. Z recently went to the cemetery at Bernie's request. Both mother and child continued to do well. Let me say a few words about Temmy's reaction to the loss of father.

The Case of Temmy

In our observational work, we found that whereas Bernie's reaction to his father's death was readily manifest in affects, in fantasy activity, and in verbalization, especially so with his mother, Temmy's reaction took quite a different form. Temmy was 6 years 5 months when her father died. She became sullen, was reserved with adults except her mother; she seemed to restrict the ebb and flow of affective experiencing, restraining feelings. She also excluded herself from the talks at home about missing Daddy, talk mostly initiated by Bernie, letting mother know she did not want to talk about it. She fared well in first grade, in peer relations, and in her relations to mother, her younger and older brothers. This state of self-protective restraint in reacting to father's death lasted about one year. Then softly, she began to slacken her resistance and joined in what by now was less painful familial experiencing of that loss. Perhaps in response to Bernie and mother's progressive integration of loss, Temmy began to ask questions about her father, revealing much distortion as to where her father was buried, and fearing that he would come back at night and more.

Because Temmy was no longer able to come regularly to our direct observational project (she was now in first grade), we were not able to follow her reactions to father's death directly. Nonetheless, I would like to suggest what factors may have contributed to her resisting (mother's help in) in work of mourning.

First, there was a characterologic tendency in Temmy to place a protective obstacle between herself and others, a tendency to pull in her pseudopods so to speak, over and above the fact that longitudinal relations with mother and a few selected others were good. I gained the impression over time that Temmy had a shyness of biobenetic origin, given its very early behavioral manifestations. This tendency expressed itself especially in her marked stranger anxiety reactions from as early as the fourth month of life, and it continued to manifest in a reserve or low-keyed response on entering into new (or stranger) situations. For years, if she had not been at the project for a couple of weeks, on returning she would stay close to mother, low-keyed, for about twenty minutes, after which she would seem acclimated and join her peers in some form of activity. Her affective baseline would then be more alert and cheerful.

Second, Temmy had entered latency and was making age-appropriate efforts to repress residual conflict-inducing feelings and fantasies surrounding her father. Thus, her mother and siblings' mourning manifestations were registered by an ego that was working in opposition to manifesting inner experiencing. Third, the influence of her still large residual oedipal relation to mother, even though its motivational dynamics were being repressed, may have made it more difficult for Temmy than Bernie to turn to her mother as he could with expression of how terribly she missed father. And fourth, the fact that Temmy was in school much of the day may have intensified her experience of separation and object loss and therewith her defense against talking about it while at the same time it lessened the opportunity to be with and talk to mother. No doubt other factors were also at work.

But I should also add that I have wondered this as well. Had Temmy been able to continue to come to our observational sessions twice a week, might her resistance to overtly mourn have yielded more than it did at home by her exposure to our talking about it in the group setting? Even though the work we did with Mrs. Z in helping her deal with Bernie led to his overtly mourning, perhaps it was not sufficient to facilitate Temmy's more overt mourning. We all know that by virtue of their establishing character defenses, some children are easier to help in this way than are others.

Working with Mother

Aware that a number of factors influenced the course of Bernie's and Temmy's morning process, given the evidence we saw, I felt strongly that mother played a large part in constructively facilitating her children's mourning. Above all, I want to underline the quite positive and well-developed relationship Mrs. Z has with her two children. Because we often witnessed the interactions between Bernie and his mother, we could ascertain how mourning facilitation occurred. By contrast, we saw much too little of the interaction between Temmy and her mother after father's death to verify the mother's reports of the process. We are also aware that the facilitating influence we could bring to the mother's efforts were also importantly based on the quite positive relationship with mutual respect, trust, and liking of one another that had developed between us. This was the gratifying by-product of several years of working together in our observational-interventional project. The mothers and children were very cooperative in our research on human development and on parenting, and we in turn answered to the best of our ability any questions the parents had regarding the meaning of their children's behaviors and their own parenting functions. Mrs. Z wanted us, the other mothers and staff, to talk about how to best help her children. She would tell us what Bernie, Temmy, and her adolescent son would say or ask, and she would tell us many of the things she would say and do. No doubt, I felt, our pointing out the importance of allowing, respecting, and tolerating her children's sadness and, above all, their anger at father's being ill so long and dying, made her able to let her own feelings surface quite openly as well. The group's response was sympathetic and some of the mothers could really express themselves very well.

Similarly, allowing, respecting, tolerating, and trying to understand her children's fantasies, distortions, and wishes facilitated Bernie's and eventually Temmy's verbalizations of these. Most influential I felt was that Mrs. Z understood the importance of her children's affective experiences, of their father-pertaining fantasies however unrealistic, and of their verbalizations. After her initial bewilderment at Bernie's unrealistic wishes, we never saw her react with startle or surprise at Bernie's distortions, his wishes, or his feelings. We emphasized many times how rewarding talking and letting the child talk, and how letting feelings come out in acceptable ways would help the children cope better and grow even from very painful experiences as this one. Over the years we worked together, we have had many examples to illustrate how talking about one's experiences helped the child adapt to even the most troublesome feelings of ambivalence toward their mothers and fathers.

We saw ample behavioral evidence of this mother—and of the other mothers grasping the meaning of it all—helping her children cope better than she initially showed she would by: 1) allowing her children to say whatever they said on this issue; 2) listening emotionally and talking emotionally to them (even with crying) with reassurance *based in reality;* 3) helping her children accept their own hostile destructive feelings and control and discharge these reasonably; 4) tolerating empathetically her children's fantasies, being attentive to exaggerations in order to help increase reality appreciation of what happened to cause father's illness and death; 5) allowing the disengagement from and the replacement, as well as the displacement of their object attachments; 6) recognizing and connecting stress events and symptom eruptions like Bernie's asthmatic episodes; 7) recognizing the importance of

allowing the almost tedious repetition of questions, resistant distortions, periods of depression, greater demands of the mother's
emotional availability; 8) respecting Temmy's inability to talk about
father's death while keeping the door open to it; and more. Just
as Mrs. Z's as well as Bernie's depression and Temmy's low-keyed
affect resonated through the rest of us—mothers, children, and
staff—so too did Mrs. Z's pleasure when she reported the first time
Temmy asked if her father was buried in back of their house, talked
about fearing his returning during the night, and asked to go to
the cemetery to see where he was buried.

CONCLUSION

It cannot be surprising that Bernie and Mrs. Z—Temmy to quite
a lesser degree at that time—grew emotionally in many aspects
of psychic functioning in the course of their joint work of mourning.
For me, the experience answers Martha Wolfenstein's (1966) question
"How (before adolescence) is mourning possible?" as well as her
"Do children mourn?" Mourning is possible when the child
experiences the loss of a primary libidinal object and is helped by
a benevolent love-object ("auxiliary ego") in the task of dealing
with that loss. I believe that this mourning can proceed in the
direction of metabolizing, by means of transmuting internalization,
identification, and working through the loss of such a critically
valued object. I do not mean simply by a *displacement* of attachment, which carries with it no work of decathexis and restructuring of the ego and the self. But, I share the view of colleagues
who, like Wolfenstein, recognize the great difficulty such a prime
loss creates for the normal young child's ego. And we saw clearly
that at the ages of 4 to 6, the ages of Bernie and Temmy at the
time of their father's death, the child's ability to mourn requires
the added capabilities, love, and support of a highly emotionally
invested auxiliary ego, the other parent. This point has been made
by both Robert and Erna Furman, but it bears repetition. In a

series of papers dating back to the 1960s, R. Furman (1964, 1973) drew attention to the central role of surviving caregivers in supporting the child's tolerance and expression of sad and angry feelings. E. Furman (1974) specified "the role of the surviving love objects in . . . presenting the realities of the event, and in serving as a model for coping with [the loss]" (pp. 239–240). Her experience led her to note that "the adults hide their own expressions of grief from the child and, *in part to protect themselves,* do not welcome manifestations of the child's affects. . . . [She] noted repeatedly that the prelatency child needed 'permission' from his surviving parent before he could . . . discharge sadness and anger in regard to object loss" (p. 261, italics added).

On the basis of this line of thought, it is critical that the auxiliary ego, the other parent, understand how to help the child mourn. That know-how can be greatly facilitated by mental health instructive interventions. But this, in turn, requires that we ourselves, as Zetzel (1965) urged, be capable of tolerating our own depression, be able to empathetically hear and feel the experiencing of the remaining parent and the child. And H. Hardin and D. Hardin (2000) may have a strong point in suggesting a further probable operative factor that stands as an obstacle to parents or ourselves helping a child mourn, which is, that "when caregivers are unable to proceed beyond a particular stage of mourning, the child's mourning process [will often be] arrested" (p. 1246). And agreeing with R. Furman, E. Furman, and H. Hardin and D. Hardin, I believe that "it is necessary for surviving family members to mourn openly in order for the bereaved child to become involved in a healthy mourning process" (Hardin and Hardin 2000, p. 1246). We cannot afford to delude ourselves about the difficulty of achieving this task. Freud (1930, Chapter 2) pointed out that we humans have made love the center of our lives, not by choice, but by virtue of the libido and our prolonged period of childhood helplessness and dependence. And he held that, as a result, we remain vulnerable, quite normally, to the reverberations within us of loss affects because none of us is able to completely resolve cathexes that, Freud (1939) held, are indelible. As is the case with helping our patients whatever the nature of their pain, we must expect to feel the stress of that pain, and that of mourning in those we help in their labor of mourning. We accept that our beloved children's birth has its labors; and so does the loss of those we love, that we labor to cathect and eventually have to labor to decathect.

REFERENCES

Bonnard, A. (1950). The mother as therapist, in a case of obsessional neurosis. *Psychoanalytic Study of the Child* 5:391–408.

Fraiberg, S. (1980). *Clinical Studies in Infant Mental Health: The First Year of Life.* New York: Basic Books.

Frank, E. and Rowe, D. (1981). Primary prevention: parent education, mother-infant groups in a general hospital setting. *Journal of Preventive Psychiatry* 1:169–178.

Fries, M.E. (1946). The child's ego development and the training of adults in his environment. *Psychoanalytic Study of the Child* 2:85–112.

Freud, S. (1909). Analysis of a Phobia in a Five-Year-Old Boy. *Standard Edition* 10:3–149.

———. (1930). Civilization and Its Discontents. *Standard Edition* 21:59–145.

———. (1939). An Outline of Psychoanalysis. *Standard Edition* 23:141–207.

Furman, E. (1957). Treatment of under-fives by way of parents. *Psychoanalytic Study of the Child* 12:250–262.

———. (1974). *A Child's Parent Dies.* New Haven, CT: Yale University Press.

Furman, R. (1964). Death and the young child: some preliminary considerations. *Psychoanalytic Study of the Child* 19:321–333.

———. (1973). A child's capacity for mourning. In *The Child in His Family: The Impact of Disease and Death* Yearbook of the International Association for Child Psychiatry and Allied Professions, Vol. 2, ed. E.J. Anthony and C. Koupernik, pp. 225–231. New York: Wiley.

Greenspan, S. (1992). *Infancy and Early Childhood.* New York: International Universities Press.

Hardin, H.T. and Hardin, D.H. (2000). On the vicissitudes of early primary surrogate mothering: Loss of the surrogate mother and arrest of mourning. *Journal of the American Psychoanalytic Association* 48:1229–1258.

Jacobson, E. (1964). *The Self and the Object World.* New York: International Universities Press.

Mahler, M. S., Pine, F. and Bergman, A. (1975). *The Psychological Birth of the Human Infant*. New York: Basic Books.

Nagera, H. (1970). Children's reactions to the death of important objects. *Psychoanalytic Study of the Child* 25:360–400.

Parens, H. (1979). *The Development of Aggression in Early Childhood*. Northvale, NJ: Jason Aronson Inc.

———. (1988). A Psychoanalytic Contribution Toward Rearing Emotionally Healthy Children: Education for Parenting. In *New Concepts in Psychoanalytic Psychotherapy*, ed. J.M. Ross and W.A. Myers, pp. 120–138. Washington, DC: American Psychiatric Press.

Parens, H. and Pollock, L. (1981). Film #6: *An Hysterical Paralysis in a Three-Year-Old Boy*. Education Media Section, The Medical College of Pennsylvania, Philadelphia, PA.

Parens, H., Pollock, L. and Prall, R.C. (1974). Film #2: *Toward an Epigenesis of Aggression in Early Childhood*. Audio-Visual Medical Section, Eastern Pennsylvania Psychiatric Institute, Philadelphia, PA.

Parens, H., Pollock, L., Stern, J. and Kramer, S. (1976). On the girl's entry into the oedipus complex. *Journal of the American Psychoanalytic Association* 24:79–107.

Provence, S. and Naylor, A. (1983). *Working with Disadvantaged Parents and Their Children*. New Haven, CT: Yale Universities Press.

Ruben, M. (1945). A contribution to the education of a parent. *Psychoanalytic Study of the Child* 1:247–261.

Singletary, W. (1993). Education for parenting. In *Prevention in Mental Health* ed. H. Parens and S. Kramer, pp. 157–166. Northvale, NJ: Jason Aronson Inc.

Spitz, R. (1965). *The First Year of Life*. New York: International Universities Press.

Wolfenstein, M. (1966). How is mourning possible? *Psychoanalytic Study of the Child* 21:93–123.

———. (1974). *The past recaptured in the work of Rene Magritte*. Presented at the 5th Annual Margaret S. Mahler Symposium, Philadelphia, PA, May 1974.

Zetzel, E.R. (1965). Depression and the incapacity to bear it. In *Drives, Affects, Behavior, 2*, ed. M. Schur, pp. 243–274. New York: International Universities Press.

9

INTERRUPTED MOURNING

Discussion of Parens' Chapter,
"An Obstacle to the Child's
Coping with Object Loss"

Theodore Fallon, Jr., M.D.

Henri Parens poses a question for us to consider: Can a child actually mourn the loss of a libidinal object? In order to properly explore this matter, it is helpful to refer to Masur (1984, pp. 52–53) who breaks this larger question down into five specific questions: At what age does loss affect the child? At what ages does the child perceive the loss? At what age does the child begin to understand death? At what age does the child begin to mourn? And what are the ego capacities that are necessary to do so? The last two questions especially concern our present inquiry though, the broader context should, of course, be kept in mind.

THE DEFINITIONS OF MOURNING

With regard to the question of the age at which a child can mourn, Masur (1984) has pointed out that the answer depends at least in part on the definition of mourning that is used. Implied and explicit definitions of mourning vary considerably in the literature.

At one end of the spectrum is Freud's (1912, p. 65) definition, which is oriented toward the outcome of mourning: "The task of mourning is to detach the survivor's memories and hopes from the dead." Anna Freud (1960, p. 58) refined this definition by stating that "mourning, taken in the analytic sense, is the individual's effort to accept a fact in the external world (the loss of the cathected object) and to effect corresponding changes in the inner world (withdrawal from the lost object)." At the other end of the spectrum, Bowlby (1960) suggests that mourning is the psychological processes set in motion by the loss of the loved object and which commonly lead to the relinquishment of the object. This definition focuses on the process much more than the outcome and allows a much broader array of responses that would easily include those processes that occur even in very young children.

Parens does not supply an explicit definition of mourning, but shows us elements of both of those cited above. For example, in the case presented by Parens, Bernie's initial reaction to his father's death is melancholia and withdrawal. He then asks his mother to take his daddy out of the ground, bring him to the hospital, and Dr. Parens could make him better. Later, he seemed to have transferred the role of "Dad" onto his friend's father. Finally, Bernie requested to visit the cemetery. This progress strongly suggests a withdrawing of cathexis from the object as Freud (1912) defined mourning.

There is also another process described in the case of Bernie that is at least as important—a developmental one. For example, Bernie struggles with the problem of how to manage his aggressive impulses toward his peer when they wrestle. This, of course, is a normal development challenge and in another context would have nothing to do with mourning. With the death of his father, however, this developmental challenge becomes all the more acute. Bernie's struggle is evidenced by his extreme withdrawal to his mother's arms after inadvertently stepping on his friend's finger while wrestling him. Four months later, however, he is boxing and carrying a gun. Again, this developmental progression suggests that the mourning process is moving along. This developmental progression fits with Bowlby's (1960) idea of mourning.

For purposes of this paper, I would like to define mourning in its broadest sense (along the lines of Bowlby) as the process that works toward coping with a loss. The aim of this coping is to readjust an understanding of the world so that it more closely matches reality. A good outcome of the mourning process is to optimize function and potential by blending previous experiences with the present reality of the loss. That is, what has been learned and experienced prior to the loss is not abandoned, but rather integrated with the new reality of the loss.

Given this definition, Parens' answer to the question, "Can the child mourn the loss of a libidinal object" is, indeed, yes a child can. Using this definition, it is easy to find other examples in the literature of children some as young as 6 months who show evidence of mourning (Aubrey 1955, Barnes 1964, Bowlby 1953, Heinicke and Westheimer 1965, Robertson and Bowlby 1952 to name a few).

REQUISITE CONDITIONS TO MOURNING

Just as with adults, however, not all children can rise to the challenges of mourning. What are the requisite conditions that allow mourning to take place for a child? Although Deutsch (1937) in her seminal paper on mourning, postulates that a child's ego is too weak to do the work of mourning, it is noteworthy that this paper presented psychoanalyses of only adults who had lost mothers during childhood and no children themselves. Furman's (1974) list of requisite conditions for mourning includes perception, memory, and object constancy. Although most recent authors have agreed with this in principle, there is some argument as to when a child has sufficient object constancy. Bowlby (1960) feels that infants as young as 6 months of age have sufficient object constancy to mourn. Furman (1964) feels this object constancy is present from the third or fourth year of life. Nagera (1970) agrees that object constancy is an important element that leads to responses in the child (protest, despair, and denial or detachment) as described by Bowlby (1961) that appear similar to those in mourning adults. However, he feels that these superficially similar responses are based on completely different reasons and mechanisms. One of his reasons for this view is that children have been noted to have a "short sadness span" (Wolfenstein 1966). Here he gives as an example that children cried when they heard of President John F. Kennedy's death, but then were impatient when they could not find their usual programs on television that evening. He concludes that children have a low capacity for the tolerance of acute pain (Nagera 1970, p. 372).

In contradiction to Nagera, however, there are examples in the literature (A. Freud and Burlingham 1944, Aubrey 1955) that note sustained moaning, crying, rage, and searching in mourning. In describing mourning children, Aubrey notes:

> Tears are often continuous, interrupted by paroxysms and short moments of respite during which the child lies exhausted in his bed. It can last for several days; some children cried almost without interruption for six or seven days. Most often the crying expresses despair . . . but despair sometimes gives way to anger. Sam, 17 months, stood in his bed, shrieking at the top of his voice without any respite and looked hostile; when he saw the observer in the distance, he went into paroxysms of rage, shook the bars of the cot and stamped his feet. His cries became even stronger and raucous and he thrust the observer away violently. . . . Despair is sometimes accompanied by yearning and anguish. . . . Most of the children who do not speak show by their attitude that they are waiting and looking for their mothers. Their eyes watch the door and when it opens they start to come out of their apathy to examine the person who comes in. If the child is walking, he wanders sorrowfully about the room

looking in corners (Aubrey as quoted by Heinicke and Westheimer 1965, p. 278).

AN OBSTACLE TO MOURNING

Parens too asks what the requisite conditions for mourning might be. Instead of focusing on the child as an independent functioning agent, however, Parens takes the lead of Winnicott (1945, 1960) who notes that no child can exist without a parent. Spitz (1945), in his observation of infants in a foundling home, notes that the child depends on the parent for developmental sustenance. Parens notes this in his reference to the parent as an auxiliary ego. He elaborates this point by examining a particular condition requisite to a child's mourning. This condition is that there is another person, usually the parent, who, as a matter of developmental course, provides an auxiliary ego to sustain the child's efforts to cope with the loss. In contrast to Nagera (1970), who feels that it is the child's "short sadness span" that limits mourning, Parens notes that it is the adult—the auxiliary ego—who turns away from the pain, and therefore may limit the child's ability to mourn. He postulates that those who would act as an auxiliary ego themselves experience pain while attempting to assist the child, implying a turning away from the discomfort. His paper provides some examples of the ways in which parents, teachers, and even therapists turn away from the painful process of mourning in the children.

Parens' initial description of adults turning away from the pain of a child's mourning implies that simply not turning away from this discomfort is sufficient to assist the child (given that there are not other impediments). In other words, simply being a parent and attending to the child's feelings rather than turning away from them allows that child to do what is necessary to integrate the loss into his reality. He provides the vignette of Bernie as an example.

If this is so, then one of Parens' contributions is to say that simply functioning as an optimal parent allows the child to proceed in a productive and perhaps successful mourning process. Restated another way, the functioning of the parent in the parent–child dyad is a necessary condition to mourning. This is yet another example of Parens' previous work that emphasizes the importance of including the parent when considering a child's development and functioning.

R. Furman (1968) agrees with this, saying that a child can mourn if given the proper support and milieu in which he will be realistically assured of the fulfillment of age-appropriate needs. He would also add that the investment of the parents or other important adults in the child and his achievements is of critical importance to the child's continuing development and as such constitutes a component of the proper support and milieu mentioned above.

In talking about an obstacle to the child's coping with object loss, Parens seems to go beyond talking of the parent as an external support. He seems to be implying that the supporting auxiliary ego is an integral part of the child's functioning: in other words, a functioning mother–child unit. The normative state of things for a child is that there is an auxiliary ego that is part of this functioning mother–child unit. And when that auxiliary ego interferes with the child mourning, there is an obstacle to the mourning process. Parens' example of Bernie attempts to demonstrate, as he says, that ". . . mother can be helped to be more effectively helpful to her child . . ." In other words, she can function more optimally as a parent. For example, prior to the father's death, Parens' comments to both Bernie and his mother about Bernie's aggression in breaking a spoon and then identifies Bernie's resultant anxiety. Parens' comments suggest that he was speaking to this mother–child unit. After the father's death, again there is an example of Parens speaking to the mother–child unit when Bernie steps on Harold's finger. Then, following a communication between Bernie and his mother ("his mother said something to him softly"), there is new material that suggests that this mother–child unit works together. With Parens' assistance, both Bernie and his mother in tandem struggle to integrate a clear understanding (and perhaps acceptance) of the loss of his father. We see this integration in Bernie by the progression of material both in direct observation and by mother's reports. We see this integration in the mother by her initial difficulties in assisting Bernie and then her reports of new material about Bernie, heralding a change in her understanding (at least of Bernie, and possibly of her husband's death). Parens' final section on working with mother lends further support to this view.

MOURNING THE EMOTIONALLY INVESTED OBJECT AND THE DEVELOPMENTAL OBJECT

Parens' paper touches on another aspect of mourning that may be useful to pursue. He alerts us to this issue when he alternately uses the terms "libidinal object" and "emotionally invested object," then later uses the term "auxiliary ego." Parens tells us that Bernie has good relatedness, with identification especially with father. There is no indication, however, that the father served much as a major auxiliary ego, though clearly, the father was a significant emotionally invested object for him. The use of the term libidinal object, however, seems to be more complex. For an adult, a libidinal object might simply refer to an emotionally invested object, while for a child, a libidinal object might include an object that is both emotionally invested and functions as an auxiliary ego.

Parens has presented a case that illustrates loss of an emotionally invested object only. In the case of Bernie, the primary caretaker (the auxiliary ego) is still present and available to help the child mourn. In presenting Bernie, Parens shows us that an optimally functioning parent is critical to the process of mourning. Muir and colleagues (1988) presents a similar case of a 4-year-old boy who has lost his father. This case, too, shows the necessity of an auxiliary ego in the mourning process. Parens also brings to light an aspect of mourning in childhood that has not been sufficiently examined in the literature. When a child loses a primary caretaker (the normative functioning auxiliary ego), the child must not only mourn the loss of an emotionally invested object, but must also cope with the loss of a real developmental object, unlike any that exist in a normal adult's life. The child has real psychological as well as physical dependence on this developmental object (unlike an adult who mourns any loss). The developmental object is not just an emotional investment; it is required for continued growth and for young children, for the continuation of life itself (Spitz 1945, 1946). Looking at mourning in this way suggests that loss of a caretaking parent for a child really contains two components: (1) the loss of an emotionally invested object, which fits in Freud's definition of the mourning process; and (2) the loss of the auxiliary ego. As with adult mourning, the case of Bernie is the loss of an emotionally invested object.

H. Hardin and D. Hardin's (2000) recent description of the loss of an early primary surrogate mother may be useful in this discussion. They note that early primary surrogates, such as an au pair, can have serious developmental consequences. This may be an examination of the loss of a developmental object that has potential to help us understand the vicissitudes of this type of loss.

But "the death of a mother is a loss like no other" (Masur, Chapter 3 of this volume). A child faced with these two simultaneous losses is like suddenly being told to go on a journey across the country and at the same time losing the vehicle that had always been available to make journeys before. Mourning the loss of a caretaking parent for a child, then, requires that the child do more than the adult: cope with the loss of an emotionally invested object *and* cope with the loss of a developmental object. This fact was overlooked in the original work on mourning in children, which failed to take into account development itself. With newer insights, such as outlined above, the contrast between mourning in children and adults quickly breaks down.

INTERRUPTED MOURNING

If we now go back and reexamine material similar to Deutsch's through the lens of development, we may notice things that we have missed before. For this purpose, I will describe material from the analysis of a 30-year-old man, A., whose family was in a house fire just before dawn when he was 20 months old. Although he had minor injuries and was released from the hospital within a day, his mother was badly injured, suffering head trauma and fractures, while his father was killed.

By reports from others and vague memories of his own, he knew that after the accident, he had initially been cared for by his maternal aunt. He recalled crying but also feeling soothed by his aunt. At some point within a year, the mother was able to resume his care, although it has not been clear exactly when that was, or how reduced his mother's ability to care for him was. The father had been an educator and the family was deeply religious. The mother interpreted the father's death as God's vengeance for being too proud and complacent. In response, A. recalls his mother's teachings that being proud and complacent was dangerous, and felt deep anxiety when these affects arose in him. A. also recalls that as he got older, he felt tremendous emptiness and anxiety at night, which frequently led to sleeplessness. During the day, he reported functioning reasonably well, including exceling in school and finally taking on his father's profession. He also noted that he was constantly trying to ask his mother questions. He recalls his mother's response was frequently, "Go talk to the walls."

He came to analysis because he noticed that he frequently felt angry, and that this anger did not seem to fit the situation in which it arose. Initially in the analysis, although there were fears of losing the analyst, these were infrequently discussed and mainly acted out around vacations and holidays. Whatever was discussed around loss seemed to have little expressed affect, and the material did not develop. The bulk of the material came in the form of transference, with repeated attempts to convince the analyst that he had the needs of a young child, and requests that the analyst provide for him the way his mother had not been able to. He was finally able to verbalize a fantasy that if the analyst could provide for him in this way, all of the anxieties that he had in the present, all of the self-destructive behaviors that he was acutely aware of would recede. It was only after considerable time working through this material, which seemed to be related to development and his relationship with his mother, was he able to begin to mourn the loss of his father. This material came up in the form of an image of sitting by the back stoop waiting for his father to return. With this image came the recognition that his father would not return and that he needed to come in the house and go to bed.

For this case, the father would seem to fit this description of an emotionally invested object much as Bernie had lost his father. The difference in this case is the A. lost his developmental object, at least temporarily if not permanently in some ways. It is also striking to note that the developmental material had to be address in the analysis before he could mourn the loss of the emotionally invested object. Similar to the way that Parens positions the auxiliary ego as an integral part of the child, in this case it seems that the developmental functions are critical to the mourning process. Once the parenting issues were addressed with Bernie's mother, mourning the loss of the father followed. In the case of A., once the developmental issues were addressed in the analysis, mourning the loss of his father, which was interrupted so long ago, resumed. It can be concluded that the analyst, through the transference, provided the auxiliary ego function necessary, which the mother, due to her absence, had not been able to, and that this facilitated a belated onset of the mourning process

CONCLUSION

Although there are many questions and disagreements with regard to the process of mourning the loss of an emotionally invested object, a coherent discussion of mourning is predicated on an agreed-upon definition. Different definitions lead to different conclusions. From a developmental perspective in which the parent–child dyad is an optimally functioning unit, Parens presents evidence that strongly suggests that a 4-year-old is capable of withdrawing cathexis from the object. An impediment to this optimally functioning dyad is the parent's own resistance to facing the discomfort of mourning themselves.

If we separate out the need to mourn the loss of an emotionally invested object from the loss of a developmental object (auxiliary ego), then it becomes clear that the task of mourning for the child may be far greater if that lost object is both the auxiliary ego as well as the emotionally invested object. Material from a brief case presentation suggests that the developmental aspects of the loss need to be attended to before other emotionally invested aspects.

REFERENCES

Aubrey, J. (1955). *La Carence de soins Maternals*. Paris: Presses Universitaires de France.

Barnes, M. (1964). Reactions to the death of a mother. *Psychoanalytic Study of the Child* 19: 334–357.

Bowlby, J. (1953). Some pathological processes set in train by early mother–child separations. *Journal of Mental Sciences* 99: 265.

————. (1960). Grief and mourning in infancy and early childhood. *Psychoanalytic Study of the Child* 15: 9–52.

————. (1961). Processes of mourning. *International Journal of Psycho-Analysis* 42:317–340.

Deutsch, H. (1937). The absence of grief. *Psychoanalytic Quarterly* 6:12–22.

Freud, A. (1960). A discussion of Dr. John Bowlby's Paper, "Grief and Mourning in Infancy and Early Childhood." *Psychoanalytic Study of the Child* 15: 53–62.

Freud, A. and D. Burlingham (1944). *Infants Without Families*. New York: International Universities Press.

Freud, S. (1912). Totem and taboo. *Standard Edition* 13:1–162.

Furman, E. (1974). *A Child's Parent Dies*. New Haven, CT: Yale University Press.

Furman, R. (1968). Additional remarks on mourning and the young child. *Bulletin of the Philadelphia Association of Psychoanalysis* 18: 124–138.

———. (1964). Death and the young child: some preliminary considerations. *Psychoanalytic Study of the Child* 19:321–333.

Hardin, H.T. and D.H. Hardin (2000). On the vicissitudes of early primary surrogate mothering: loss of the surrogate mother and arrest of mourning. *Journal of the American Psychoanalytic Association* 48: 1229–1258.

Heinicke, C.M. and Westheimer, I. (1965). *Brief Separations*. New York: International Universities Press.

Masur, C. (1984). Early childhood bereavement: theoretical and clinical considerations. *Clinical Psychology*. Vol. 4, p. 224.

Muir, E., Speirs, A., and Tod, G. (1988). Family intervention and parental involvement in the facilitation of mourning in a 4–year-old boy. *Psychoanalytic Study of the Child* 43: 367–383.

Nagera, H. (1970). Children's reactions to the death of important objects—a developmental approach. *Psychoanalytic Study of the Child* 25: 360–400.

Robertson, J. and Bowlby, J. (1952). A two-year-old goes to the hospital. *Psychoanalytic Study of the Child* 7: 82–94.

Spitz, R. (1945). Hospitalism—an inquiry into the genesis of psychiatric conditions in early childhood. *Psychoanalytic Study of the Child* 1: 53–74.

———. (1946). Hospitalism—a follow-up report on investigation described in volume I, 1945. *Psychoanalytic Study of the Child* 2: 113–117.

Winnicott, D. (1945). Primitive emotional development. *International Journal of Psycho-Analysis* 26: 137–143.

———. (1960). The theory of the parent–infant relationship. *International Journal of Psycho-Analysis* 41: 585–595.

Wolfenstein, M. (1966). How is mourning possible? *Psychoanalytic Study of the Child* 21: 93–123.

10

THE MOURNING AFTER
A Concluding Overview

M. Hossein Etezady, M.D.

Loss and mourning as ubiquitous and universal plights in human experience spare no one. It is the existential lot of the human being to seek and long for the magical bliss of omnipotence and the promise of a utopian contentedness and imperturbable security, while menaced by an unending barrage of internal and external disturbance and threats of disruption, helplessness, and loss of control. Every developmental progression and age-specific task represents such an upheaval, containing loss, requiring and inducing a process of mourning that paves the way for change, reorganization, and gain in the form of added strength and new capabilities.

Since it is not possible to shield our lives against the impact of the inevitable, the question to be asked is how we endure the pain and how we manage to process the mourning after each loss and experience the life-altering consequences that ensue.

Mother, as the original object of libidinal attachment, provides the anchor, the shield and the magical source of the narcissistic omnipotence that establishes and maintains a background of safety and constancy needed for the maturation of ego resources and individuation of the dependent infant (Spitz 1965, Mahler et al. 1975, Akhtar 1994). This oceanic bliss of the symbiotic period persists as the distant memory of a lost paradise, forever beckoning and beguiling, yet only rarely, fleetingly, and illusively realized. As the child individuates, the main challenge of development is contained in the task of "hatching" and separating out of this ideal illusion of perfect contentedness and constancy. This is an increasingly complex task in a challenging arena of unsettling needs, demands, consequences, and frequent frustrations. As the new toddler buoyantly and enthusiastically grapples with each new step and reaches for new horizons, intoxicated by the thrill of mastery and the rewards of practicing, he moves slowly but irretrievably away from this illusion of omnipotence and dual unity with the symbiotic partner. Denial of the separation, rage, protest, and coercive attempts to recapture the lost paradise only increase the distance, deepen the anxiety, and intensify the dread of the loss of the mother or her love. Mother, when able to sustain her own libidinal availability while weathering the storm, enables the child to bear this irrefutable loss in manageable doses. She helps him overcome the disorganization caused by the affective storms of rage and despondency through holding and containment of the upheaval in the wake of his organismic panic.

Mother's empathic attunement and intuitive recognition of the child's complicated internal states and her restorative responses sustain the child as he begins to develop his own internal resources and means of affective modulation, resiliency, and his own creative solutions. It is in the process of this intersubjective engagement that the capacity for mourning and coping with loss, adversity, and frustration is cultivated. Mother's empathic appreciation of the uniqueness of her child's emotional universe and his state of mind becomes the mirror that objectifies his experience and lays the foundation for subjective reflection. The capacity to mourn, reorganize, and move on involves an enormously complicated and intricate process that draws upon every essential aspect of optimal development. When this capacity is not adequately established, the future course of self-organization, object relations, personality, and development is at risk.

MEYERS' CONTRIBUTION

In Chapter 2, Helen Meyers, using Freud's (1917) classical model of identification with the lost object and Bowlby's stages of grief and its resolution, succinctly and clearly summarizes the psychological process of mourning in its theoretical essence. She notes that Freud's model features decathexis and identification while Bowlby's (1961) stresses yearning and attempt at retrieval. The final outcome in both these views is reorganization and moving on.

Having summarized the theoretical aspects of the mourning process in these terms, Meyers proceeds to present her own original contribution: the intriguing notion that mourning the loss of the mother in the adult woman entails unique and specific features. These features, she contends, are not observable when the adult woman loses her father, nor when a man loses his mother. In her elaboration of this contention, she explains that a woman never completely separates from her mother in the course of separation-individuation. The oedipal resolution and the passing of adolescence strengthen the identification of the girl with her mother, while as an external object, the mother continues to serve a self-object function and an aspect of the woman's self-representation (Kohut 1978). This is in contrast to the male child whose gender identity and self-representation grow out of disidentification with the mother. With the resolution of the Oedipus complex the male gender identity, in contrast to the female, is formed on the basis of identification with the father. Identification with the father is further reinforced during the course of adolescence.

Disidentification with the mother is not a necessary step in the formation of a female identity as it is in the case of the male child. The loss of the mother in women, reasons Meyers, is experienced as the loss of the self and causes a disruption in the organization of the self and essential self–object functions that are the vestiges of the early mother–child dyad. Whereas the loss of the father, Meyers asserts, is experienced by adult women as the loss of the "other," the loss of the mother is experienced as the loss of a part of her self. This loss is followed by subsequent alterations of major magnitude in self-representation that set in motion important changes in personality, resulting from identification with the lost object.

While the notion of the mother–daughter joint identity, incomplete separation, and absence of disidentification with the mother during the girl's early development are among our familiar theoretical concepts, the reader might nevertheless feel entitled to a healthy dose of skepticism regarding a statement as unequivocally asserted as that proposed here. Convincing, or at least plausible, evidence would be required in the form of direct clinical observation documenting these specific features. An examination of Meyers' clinical report would have to yield incontrovertible support or self-evident findings beyond the arbitrary boundaries of theoretical speculation.

To the ample satisfaction of this reader, Meyers presents such clear evidence in a direct and convincing manner in her case reports of three disparate treatment situations. These accounts are briefly yet richly illustrated. The main components of her assertions are individually demonstrated and formulated in each of these three dissimilar cases. She traces the process by which the sense of loss of part of the self subsequent to the death of a woman's mother is resolved through internalization and identification with the mother. This leads to the constitution of a permanent new internal image and libidinal attachment. Along with this comes the formation of a stronger and more complete self-image as a result of internal reorganization. She considers, examines, and deductively eliminates alternative conclusions that might seem reasonable in a casual view absent the benefit of a scrupulously illuminating psychoanalytic lens. At the conclusion of her case presentations and well-documented discussion of her findings, one finds Meyers' propositions well-supported and her contribution fully substantiated.

In her second point of contention, Meyers takes issue with the often-cited notion that as a normal part of mourning, cathexis needs to be removed from the lost object so that freed up energies can be invested in new objects. She reminds us that the hydraulic model of psychic energy supplying one object at the expense and depletion of another does not hold in our present-day view of object relationships. It is in fact a common experience that interest in or love affair with a new person increases rather than diminishes internal resources.

This may be a good juncture at which to address the question of letting go and accommodation to loss as necessary components of the process of moving on and reaching a state of reorganization that results in a new level of homeostatic equilibrium.

In grief, it is the pain of the tear in the ego that results in detachment, withdrawal, and agonizing preoccupation with the internal disturbance that consumes so much energy and creates such a consuming upheaval. This internal preoccupation and recoiling is sometimes referred to as a narcissistic withdrawal. While pathological narcissism is often a source of concern which has engendered considerable literature, we often lose sight of normal narcissism in self-organization, regulation of self-esteem, and object relations.

In this connection, I have elsewhere (Etezady 1965) explicated the significance and usefulness of delineating so-called primary narcissism from secondary narcissism. Here I would reiterate only briefly that primary narcissism refers to the mode of self-organization that prevails in the early preoedipal period, before the formation of ego boundaries or differentiation of self from object, internal from external, and wishes from reality. During this time, secondary process thinking, self and object constancy, and much of the autonomous ego capacities have not yet developed. Regulation of self states and homeostatic equilibrium of the internal conditions rely wholly on the symbiotic relationship with the mother and on the illusion of dual unity with the omnipotent object, which at this level is the ultimate prototype of a purely narcissistic self object.

Secondary narcissism by contrast is a by-product of separation–individuation that evolves in a gradual manner beginning after differentiation and through the rapprochement subphase and its resolution. It then proceeds on a course of consolidation after the beginning of self and object constancy. Like the reality principle and secondary process thinking, secondary narcissism gains normative dominance and functional integrity after the resolution of the Oedipus complex and following the structural consolidation of the ego, superego, and ego ideal (Freud 1914). Regulation of self states and self-esteem are at this time dependent on the adequacy and relative maturation of these structures. While external sources of narcissistic replenishment remain vital, the mode of relatedness to the object is now determined by internalized working models of relationships that have been abstracted and relatively depersonified. Mutuality, empathic attunement, and realistic assessment of the mind of others have become available as instruments of social engagement and interaction.

This higher mode of relatedness based on achievement of self and object constancy is the consequence of what Freud (1914) termed secondary narcissism. He defined secondary narcissism as the withdrawal of the libido from the object (of primary narcissism) and reinvesting this libidinal energy in the self-representation that we now view as "hatching" out of an intersubjective matrix containing "metabolized introjects" and "internal working models." This is the process that results in the progressive differentiation of self from the object, gradual relinquishment of infantile omnipotence, and incremental deidealization of the object into more realistic dimensions. The transition from omnipotence and grandiosity to the capacity for realistic assessment of self and other is possible when the weaning process is gradual and gentle, in manageable doses, and in an atmosphere of libidinal constancy, maternal attunement, and empathy. The essential ingredient here is the caregiver's ability to hold and to contain the toxic affective storms that create splitting and polarity. "Good-enough mothering" is the crucial element necessary to neutralize destructive aggression through libidinization of the relationship for the child. This precisely is the challenge of the rapprochement subphase in every mother–child relationship in order to heal the split, integrate affective polarity of self and object states, and sepa-rate the internal from the external sources of influence. This lays the groundwork for achieving a sense of control and constancy in relationships through trial identification and empathic resonance. Sudden disruption, unmanageable upheavals, extremes of ambivalence, maternal apathy, sustained and extreme depriva-tion, or severe deflation of infantile omnipotence are inimical to the notion of "good enough" in the quality of experience and caregiving.

To traverse this important developmental course, that is, moving from the subjective state of primary narcissism to the object-related state of self-regulation in the form of secondary narcissism, many prerequisites have to be met. Not all children have the good fortune of making this transition unscathed and free of pathologi-cal vicissitudes of narcissism. In theory, those who do reach this level of optimal integrity with its ego-specific features have suc-ceeded in relinquishing the object of primary narcissism painfully, gradually, and repeatedly in the context of numerous mutative interactions and acts of fate. They have gained through these losses via identification and internalization. They have retained the ab-stracted essence of their past object relations' experiences in the matrix of a transforming intersubjective universe. This paves the way for the capacity to endure and gain from future losses that are unavoidable and generate unforeseen storms of pain, rage, and disturbing upheaval. Here, loss can lead to constructive change, reorganization, increase in strength, wisdom, and novel modes of coping with demands of reality from within as well as without. Relinquishing and successfully mourning the loss of the object of the primary narcissism era, and moving into the secondary mode of narcissism are essential prerequisites of self and object constancy. This is, in essence, the transition from the paranoid–schizoid position to the depressive position. It establishes the capacity to mourn as a means of moving on, in time, on a journey within oneself, yet in exquisite connection resonating with the subjective sensibilities of significant others. Without this capacity to mourn and reorganize, emotional growth is indeed arrested and no movement beyond the early affective storms of the rapprochement crisis is feasible.

When our older theoretical models stress the need for relinquishing the lost object as a final resolution in mourning, we are reminded that this dictum applies to the developmental task of moving beyond the mode of object relationship inherent in primary narcissism. When we lose parents, friends, lovers, teachers, and leaders, we can bear this loss as we build and live in a world of their memories, cherish their legacy, gain solace in reminiscences, and find comfort in treasuring momentos. We visit their graves, display their pictures, and wistfully share our remembrances of them. They remain a part of us, sometimes more compellingly after their demise, and become a permanent part of who we are, how we live, and what we dream.

As for the question of confronting children with death, loss, and traumatic affective states that they may not be able to tolerate, I believe our standards of analytic technique provide the answer. We meet the child's ego where we find it. We follow the child's lead, rather than lead his material. We use developmental considerations in judging the child's need for his defenses. Clarification, confrontation, and interpretations are gauged at the level of the defenses and the child's state of readiness. Identifying, naming, clarifying, and connecting the affects to behavior and sequence of events are the bread and butter of analytic treatment. We expand the child's ego resources, pave the way for the next inevitable step, delicately and compassionately, mindful of the impact of our interventions and carefully guarding against any possibility of creating a trauma.

SCHLESINGER'S CONTRIBUTION

Schlesinger's contribution (Chapter 6) on analyzing the mourning patient is at once common sense and intuitively obvious, yet at the same time eminently illuminating and far-reaching in its implications. Although the issues he addresses are multifaceted and complicated, his insightful and incisive points of technique are lucidly discussed and are presented in a manner that renders them readily applicable and highly valuable in clinical practice. Schlesinger highlights a variety of resistances to mourning as an affective experience. When these resistances are not recognized, the whole process of mourning can be derailed and the presentation of the analytic material and its manifest text becomes confusing as the progress in the analytic work is stalled. The finality of loss and its acceptance evokes more resistance than any other factor.

While the points of technique are elaborated in the context of the analysis of adults, Schlesinger's stated concern about understanding, tolerating, and the appreciation of the mourning process as an indispensable and valuable aspect of development apply no less aptly in the case of children. In children in particular, the notion of finality remains unfathomable well into early adolescence. Because of the pain, rage, helplessness, guilt, and shame that may be the main components of the unbearable emotional onslaught, powerful protective defenses will be erected. Guilt and self-blame by themselves can energize the machinery driving the resistances and result in denial, avoidance, or minimizing the impact of the loss. When guilt is compelling and its grip overwhelming, its acknowledgment becomes unbearable and its existence is concealed from conscious awareness. Despair, self-loathing, loss of interest, and anxious self-torment can disguise the unconscious guilt fueled by disavowed sadistic impulses. Any other affective charge of unbearable intensity can create resistance and emergency defenses that serve to protect the individual from feeling overwhelmed. This is seen more often and far more readily in children due to their limited ego resources and less mature defensive capabilities. Overactivity, either in physical-motor manifestation or in make-believe fantasy, play, and distractibility are common and familiar reactions in children to unpleasant and distasteful affective states. As Schlesinger aptly and repeatedly points out, it is not that we disapprove of resistances and regard them as undesirable constructs impeding progress. We appreciate and respect the resistances for the important protection that they provide. We seek to understand what this protection is guarding against.

Resistance to recognition and living through the painful affects can also originate from the side of the analyst and may result in complete derailment of the course of the treatment. The therapist may become intolerant or dismissive of the affective outpour, become bored or impatient with the mourning process, and regard the patient's preoccupation with mourning and grief as insignificant or not worthy of the inordinate time that it might consume. The emotional upheaval of mourning tends to be episodic and the profound effects of a traumatic loss are never fully abated. As Schlesinger states, mourning comes in waves, rising and dissipating. This cannot be taken for resistance against accepting the loss, since this is nature's way of allowing for healing and reorganization. Keeping a stiff upper lip and suppressing the natural process of mourning, which may be valued by some social and cultural standards, are but obstacles to the process of working-through in treatment. Schlesinger's emphasis is well worth repeating, that from a technical point of view, it is better to err on the side of treating the extended expression of grief as a normal process rather than assuming it to be a manifestation of refusing to accept the inevitable. Caution is advised against the tendency "to do something" in order to spare the patient the pain of his suffering. Inappropriate interpretative intervention or providing support when it is not needed, offered with the intent to convey empathy, is no more than mere "meddling." Patients may need reassurance to allow mourning to run its natural course and reassurance that there is no need to interrupt the emotional outpouring in an attempt to control it.

Schlesinger's technical gems are polished by many years of distinguished clinical experience and presented in the best of the psychoanalytic tradition and practice. He reminds us that loss is an inevitable aspect of every life, that mourning is a natural response to loss, and he warns us against pathologizing it in our clinical practice. He makes clear how and why mourning must take time and take its own physiological course. Our task is to respect, appreciate, and witness the process, not to meddle and not to impede or discourage its progress. We help our patients when we tolerate, appreciate, and understand the emotions and defenses, and the purpose these defenses serve. If the mourning process is impeded, resolution and integration of the experience will be hindered and treatment objectives will be obscured.

Regarding the application of object relations principles and developmental concepts of self-organization to the analytic treatment of adults in the process of mourning (Settlage 1989), I believe the maternal and self-object functions of holding, containment, and being a transforming object well characterize the role and posture of the analyst. These principles apply to child care as they do to analytic work with the young or in treating adults, especially in dealing with the loss of a love object.

Schlesinger defines and distinguishes between loss of a part of one's self, loss of a loved one, and the sense of loss in the process of analytic treatment. The latter is encountered as the patient abandons one position in favor of a new one that is more adaptive. This sense of loss becomes more compelling as the analysis approaches termination and the patient faces imminent loss of the analyst. It requires special attention, ongoing scrutiny, and working through. I can only amplify what Schlesinger clearly and articulately explicates: that loss is an inherent component of developmental progression and of moving on. It is an unavoidable ingredient of emotional growth, a requirement of adaptation and a part of conforming to reality. It is an acquired capacity that is attained in the context of the first relationship, rooted in attachment, relatedness, mutuality, and being connected to others in an empathic bond. When this foundation has not been established, the capacity to mourn fails to develop, infantile omnipotence is not relinquished, and the depressive position cannot be reached. Self-object functions and relations are arrested at the level of primary narcissism, as self and object constancy do not enter the picture.

When we treat such developmentally arrested patients, we need to appreciate the extent of such developmental deficit and provide the complimentary auxiliary ego functions of the maternal transference through mirroring and holding containment that foster the gradual process of neutralization of primitive aggression. We help the patient process and progressively tolerate loss in the transference. As the affects become more manageable and subject to modulation, they can be used as guiding signals that aid self-organization and maintain internal homeostasis. This paves the way for the establishment of a coherent internal dialogue and the capacity for constructive negotiation within a dyadic context with mutuality and reciprocal responsiveness.

SETTLAGE'S CONTRIBUTION

Settlage is intimately familiar with Mahler's concepts, her research, and her theory of separation–individuation. He has worked with Mahler's theories and has explained, clarified, and expanded them in many of his previous writings and presentations. In Chapter 4, he depicts Mahler's line of vision beginning with the affective states of early infancy and the mother's corresponding reactions beginning with the child's initial solipsistic state through various phases of relatedness and beyond the resolution of rapprochement crisis. He explains that when aggression is not tolerated within the mother–child dyadic coexistence, its primitive intensity remains unmanageable and continues to threaten to destroy the self and the object. The threat of self-destruction is initially experienced as dissolution or disintegration of the self. With the advent of differentiation and demarcation of self and object boundaries by about 15 to 18 months, the inadequately neutralized aggression threatens annihilation of the object and retaliation in the form of abandonment or being destroyed. We might also add that anal sadistic drive derivatives at first and later genital oedipal elements enter the picture. By this time the ego, superego, and ego ideal have added their specific structural contributions to the developmental course of aggression.

Settlage identifies repression as the defense mechanism that keeps at bay the dangers associated with the destructive aggression. While the remaining of Settlage's description of the pitfalls and asymptomatic manifestations of repressed aggression are masterfully and clearly detailed, I find the inclusion of repression as the major mode of defensive operation during the first two years of development as implausible. Repression is possible only some time after resolution of rapprochement when the vertical split within the self and object representations has healed and sufficient neutralization of aggression has taken place (Kernberg 1975). As a result of drive fusion, the beginnings of affect modulation and self-containment have been established. Signal anxiety is now available as a sensitive instrument of constant surveillance, monitoring and meeting contingencies of homeostatic equilibrium. Repression as a more mature level of ego operation has now replaced splitting, which had heretofore been the main remedy in contending with negative affects and internal threats of primitive aggression.

In Settlage's longitudinal account of the ontogenesis of aggression, no distinction is implied between the "pre-objectal" state of primary narcissism on the one hand, and the later preoedipal period through and beyond the rapprochement subphase, on the other hand. I believe it is important and necessary to draw a clear distinction between these two different modes of relatedness and self-regulation The lasting legacy of rapprochement and its optimal resolution is the movement from primary narcissism to the mode of secondary narcissism, transition from the schizoid to the depressive position, and from a dyadic to a triadic level of interaction and conflict resolution, based on the foundation of self and object

constancy. The defenses employed against the danger of aggression
are not the same in the so-called pre-objectal phase of ego development as they are in the later part of preoedipal and oedipal
periods. While aggression in both phases may be fended off via
splitting, dissociation, or repression, for reasons set forth earlier, we
cannot speak of repression as the ego's main mechanism of defense
before the resolution of the rapprochement crisis and the consoli-
dating period that follows.

While Settlage places an exclusive focus on aggression as a
component of preoedipal development, the role of libidinal drives
cannot be ignored in the course of the unfolding of events that
pertain to aggression. During the process of neutralization that the
aggressive drives are to undergo, they lose the extreme intensity
of their negative valence and hence their destructive potential as
they are "fused" with libidinal derivatives. In this process, mother
supplies the essential ingredient of "libidinization" during the
course of each interaction via her own libidinal availability invigo-
rated by the positive charge that she gains in caring for her baby.
As she fuels the process with her own libidinal energy and loving
engagement, she is rewarded by the enriching stimulation of the
child's reinforcing response, which replenishes her own libidinal
and narcissistic resources. When in the final balance, the libidinal
charge in the mix exceeds aggression, the outcome will tend
toward progression and cohesion. Integration due to fusion results
in neutralization of aggression and enrichment of ego resources.

When the mother's ability to "libidinize" the experience for
the child is absent or insufficient, aggression remains in its primitive destructive state and triggers polarization. The purely pleasurable self and object experiences, along with their corresponding
ego states, are split off from the affective experiences of a purely
negative charge, which are projected and never integrated. Consequently, an integrated stable self-state cannot be attained and
separation between the self and object representation does not
occur. Mood states remain unmodulated and the signal function
of affects does not form. Splitting persists as the prevalent defensive

mode. Infantile omnipotence and symbiotic fantasies cannot be relinquished. Primary narcissism is not left behind. Self and object constancy are not established and the depressive position cannot be obtained. Empathic attunement and mentalization as essential tools of successfully assessing interpersonal contexts will be absent.

In this highly condensed version of what is well known about early development, I wish to stress three points. First, libidinal strivings are often thwarted by shame and guilt or a sense of vulnerability and by narcissistic depletion or injury. A mother's libidinal availability may also be affected by illness, stress, depression, anger, and early developmental deficit, arrest, or insult. This will then interfere with separation–individuation and ego development. Second, in the analytic relationship, the appreciation of libidinal components can be affected by the same factors on both sides of the couch, manifested both in the transference as well as the countertransference and also the "real relationship" between the two participants. Third, libidinal events and their expressions are subject to various degrees of inhibition or unconscious censorship in public discussions, writings, and reports for many of the reasons mentioned above, as well as the omnipresent and inviolable boundaries of privacy and confidentiality. Libidinal expressions in all cultures are universally subject to rules of propriety and are strictly censored within the tacit and unconsciously guarded boundaries of privacy that are seldom recognized or deliberately addressed. This is a consideration related to but separate from the requirements of confidentiality that we consciously and carefully observe.

The socioculturally sanctioned standard of privacy is a decisive but unspoken element that prevents us from publicly exposing our libidinally driven strivings and affective experiences with our patients. Consequently, this aspect of our clinical material seldom sees the light of day. The analytic engagement is, of course, interpersonal, but even more so, it is exquisitely personal and weaves into the deepest and most intimately private aspect of our libidinal and narcissistic reverberations. For this reason, the libidinal sector of our involvement during our work is often treated with respect and diffidence and is almost totally excluded from public exposure.

In Settlage's presentation and his exquisite case reports, we are presented with a rare glimpse of the illuminating and sensitive statements of an interpretive nature that are as integrative as they are mutative. In each instance, the patient assimilates the offering and then gratefully submits with more receptivity for the next sensitively measured input. Holding, mirroring, and containment are ample, sustained, and predictable. The analyst's libidinal availability robustly fills the background. Although we do not receive a deliberate accounting, we cannot help but feel and admire the unstated presence and the warm glow of the libidinal fuel generously provided by the analyst. Empathic attunement is ever present and center stage in every step, as close to an ideal state as any person-to-person interaction can reasonably provide. The analyst tunes in, understands, and then accepts, while reaching and presenting a fresh perspective. From this the analysand learns to understand, accept, and create a new meaning so that he can seek and discover new means.

Problems of enactment and countertransference are not addressed in this presentation, but hold a critical place, especially with patients who come from such traumatic backgrounds as in these individuals. Our patients try to teach us about their lives by making us into their ideal objects or the persecutory demons of their past. We experience and yield to this pressure in varying degrees in the service of containment and auxiliary-ego functions. In our analytic neutrality countertransference becomes a tool for deeper exploration of the unconscious processes that emanate from the analysand and influence our unconscious. When the analyst maintains a "neutral" or objective position, he can present a perspective that can open new doors for him as well as for the patient. This is the alternative to reactions or enactments that merely repeat the past and can therefore not allow for development and moving on.

PARENS' CONTRIBUTION

Parens' contribution (Chapter 8) to the present topic is a convincing and effective presentation, containing substantial issues that are often argued both in terms of theory and matters of technique. He describes and elucidates the process of mourning, not only normatively and developmentally, but also as a consequence of trauma as in the case of permanent loss of a parent. He fascinates and teaches us as he teaches and soothes the parents whose children he treats, studies, and describes.

As Parens clarifies the process of mourning and identifies children's emotional capacities and age-specific responses, the mothers become more effective instruments of developmental assistance and are able to function more competently as their child's auxiliary ego. This, it should be noted, occurs in the clear context of "mothering the mother," in the sense of empathically appreciating her needs and feeling states in order to help her deal with her own questions and with the source of her own pain. As the mother finds a supportive source of empathic attunement reliably available, she thrives on it, and her capacity to resonate with her child in empathic appreciation of his baffling emotional states is enhanced in leaps and bounds. The mutually gratifying flow of the give-and-take between the teacher and student is rich and refreshing, the engagement appears warm and comfortable, and the trusting relationship seems to be fully infused with confident expectation. To state this in terms from another dimension, the transference and countertransference are decidedly positive and charged with ample quantities of libidinal investment. The working alliance is firm and vibrant. The outcome, as one would expect and hope, is excellent and, for us, as the secondhand witnesses, reassuringly heartwarming.

Parens skillfully and systematically demonstrates his highly polished technique as he encourages, coaches, and cognitively instructs the mothers and their children to sustain their efforts in dealing effectively with their searing pain, rage, fear, shame, and guilt. At every step and without a moment's lapse, the supportive posture and compassionate regard for the subjects' vulnerability pervades. Valuable for us as vicarious participants is the special care that is taken to recognize and respond to the cognitive level that is at the child's disposal at any given point during his psychosexual development. While at a certain age a child believes it possible that a dead parent could come back to life if the child had the means or would wish it, he also may think that his anger can harm or cause the death of a loved one. Omnipotence and related fantasies, guilt, oedipal strivings, and affect tolerance are explained and fleshed out. More intriguingly, the resolution of symptomatic difficulties based on these issues are traced with impressive clarity and narrated in plain conversational language. We witness a vivid picture of how the mother and, in time, the child go through each barrier, settling one issue after another. What is not noted or described is the more personal and human aspect of the contribution on the part of the professionals and the devotion in their work, which is routinely taken for granted.

While in most instances, adults are capable of fulfilling the demanding requirements of devotion, a young child is not. Mothers, in particular, are generally considered as the epitome of devotion as a virtue of mythological proportions, an ideal that is often extended to the stereotypical image of caregivers, nurses, and physicians, among others. While members of all these groups are expected to be heroic in their devotion, their cultural heroic stereotypes are stripped of their basic human quality and inescapable frailty. Ironically, these individuals are frequently disregarded and unappreciated as living, vulnerable human beings even while they are held in awe and high respect in their sociocultural roles.

But devotion to the well-being of others has its own developmental line (A. Freud 1946). It is formed out of secure attachment to an object of libidinal constancy. It requires the timely formation of internal structures that are heir to optimal separation-individuation and derive from the ability to find reward and gratification in bringing fulfillment and solace to others as a matter of identification with one's own benevolent parents. What begins at the outset as attachment and dependency, in due course is transformed into altruistic devotion. The dependent child responds and thrives vigorously in reaction to libidinal gratification, best provided by a caregiver whose own libidinal gratification allows for emotional availability and devoted engagement. This reciprocal stimulation serves as an energizing current for those care providers who have experienced this invigorating engagement as dependent participants during their own early history, which is now encoded indelibly in their procedural memory. Having experienced libidinal object constancy, they can easily provide the same experience for a child or those whose care depends on them.

For Parens' mothers and their children, the libidinal constancy that becomes manifest in the unyielding devotion of these professionals is the critical ingredient of the chemistry that yields such remarkably impressive results. Grief, however, is inordinately taxing and consumes enormous amounts of energy. It is draining and hard to bear. The mind can best deal with its intensity and pervasive grip piece by piece and in the course of a considerable period of time. Being exposed to a grieving individual is similarly painful and can be severely taxing and demanding.

Without sustained assistance and a chance to refuel and regroup, some mothers, caregivers, or therapists may not have the capacity to deal with such a relentless drain on their emotional resources. In the process of identifying with the mournful child or patient, dormant conflicts over dependency, loss, and unresolved experiences of trauma can be awakened along with stout defenses against the awareness of the overwhelming affects. This interferes with the auxiliary-ego functions that are crucially required in child care as in therapeutic intervention. When a mother or a therapist is able to find a means of alleviating their own conflicts or replenishing their depleted emotional resources, they can serve this auxiliary-ego function better. A mother or a therapist cannot be adequately empathic or emotionally available when in a state of mind in which the internal signals are unbearable and therefore need to be shut off.

Even though we have here emphasized focusing on the affective content and allowing the flow of emotions without hindrance, we should be mindful of the importance of the need for restorative solitude. In addition to support and availability of external libidinal resources, the broken heart and the unsettled mind need solitude and secure isolation to engage in self-healing and self-soothing. These include various devices that range from autoerotic behavior to the use of various forms of transitional objects and transitional phenomena, including creative activity. These measures help reestablish a sense of cohesion, coherence, and mastery by turning the passive into active and exercising a modicum of control in a circumstance of helplessness. For children in particular, finding privacy and the opportunity to engage in self-soothing and symbolic play may not always be easy. Finding privacy can be difficult at times when adults are unduly intrusive or excessively hovering. Children may feel that adults can read their minds, or that their thoughts are transparent to others.

As mourning and grief draw upon such a vast array of emotional and intrapsychic elements, their manifestations are exquisitely personal and involve the deepest levels of a person's private universe. They reach far into the soul and the innermost depths of the individual's internal world. Individuals in grief feel unusually vulnerable and in need of a sense of safety and unconditional support. The professionals who deal with groups or individuals who are victims of loss or trauma are similarly highly vulnerable and function more effectively when they, too, are able to rely on the availability and support from co-workers, colleagues, and mentors.

CONCLUDING REMARKS

The contributors to this volume have brought to us the enormous benefit of their collective knowledge in allowing us a glimpse of their individual experience. Their expert guidance and sage mentorship is a source of comforting enlightenment and added confidence. For those of us in the healing professions who share some aspect of the work in this field, their generosity and candor are causes for gratitude as they open to us the private world of their caring devotion to the well-being of the vulnerable children and adults we all try to reach.

Reviewing the presentations of the authors contributing to this volume has been very rewarding and a source of personal pleasure. Learning about the rich experiences, the expert counsel, and carefully considered views of such a distinguished group of psychoanalytic clinicians has indeed been illuminating. I have expressed my own views at various points in order to clarify or expand a few aspects of the material under discussion. In considering loss and the mourning after each experience that brings bereavement and grief, extensive use has been made of concepts of object relations and the normative lifelong dependence that characterizes human existence. From a perspective of internal organization serving autonomy, achievement of self and object constancy is the indispensable developmental milestone reached through the separation-individuation process. While the symbiotic mode of relatedness will permanently cast its long shadow on the self-object functions and needs that sustain us through our lifetime, we aspire to live as self-directed independent individuals in charge of our own destiny, free from the interferences of external forces and the control of their powerful influence.

To this bipolar view of dependence versus autonomy, here I will add a statement with respect to the establishment of boundaries in developmental progression, as in regression. When regression is utilized in the service of the ego, it provides for a creatively flexible transition from one stage to another, as seen in play, fantasy, dreams, and problem solving, as well as in the analytic situation, among many.

Separation-individuation as a process begins an extended course that establishes and consolidates the boundaries between the self and the object. The clarity and sharp definition of these

boundaries are important requirements for internal
and homeostatic regulation that depend on stability an[d]
of self and object representations.

Not only id and ego, conscious and unconscious,
external, fantasy and reality, but self and object, yes and
and mental, past and present, as well as pain and pleasur[e]
to the distinguishing and discriminative attributes of t[he]
aries. Primary process versus secondary process thin[king]
as primary narcissism versus secondary narcissism
distinguished and differentiated within the discriminati[on]
of these boundaries.

Although well-defined and distinct, these bo[undaries]
permeable and interpenetrable as the ego's synthetic f[unction]
access the contents of each area and the so-called tran[sition]
between them. Boundaries may entail areas of over[lap]
or fusion. They may be, at times, or in places, mutua[lly]
repelling or impenetrable.

If we think of phases of development or challe[nges]
steps, challenges, or obstacles to be put behind, ea[ch]
represents a new boundary to be traversed, be it i[n]
intrapsychic, age specific, cultural, or self-imposed. C[rises]
may be random events dictated by fate.

Many factors can determine the ability of an
pass these thresholds; they can also influence the
tures of the outcome. As developmental prototypes
ements, in isolation or combined, are at work, subs[erving]
the process of separation–individuation. An importan[t]
process and its culmination in the resolution of the r[approchement]
crisis entails establishing, testing, negotiating and tr[aversing here]
tofore nonexistent boundaries. The acquisition of
forms the foundation upon which resiliency and
based. It brings together the multitude of strands th[at]
support the mechanisms and structures involved i[n]
self-regulation. From here on, contending with ev[ery chal]
lenge, living through each crisis, and surviving any

individual is incapable of utilizing the
ment in the service of repair and integ[ration]

Loss and mourning, as critical and
may be confronted at any age. The e[ffects]
affliction can be searched by questionin[g]
have combined with what quality of inna[te]
the individual for this impact. What are
of those supportive elements that may
tainment, reorganization, and recovery? H[ow]
ability to bring about or to use such fa[cilitating]
versing these, as all other developmental
will be a matter of recapitulation of separat[ion]
is the developmental dyadic template fo[r]

REFERENCES

Bowlby, J. (1961). Process of Mourning. *International J[ournal]* 340.

Etezady, M.H. (1995). Narcissism: primary-secondary, f[...] *Vulnerable Child, Vol. 2,* ed. T. Cohen, M.H. Etez[ady...] York: International Universities Press.

Freud, A. (1946). *The Ego and the Mechanisms of Defens[e...]* versities Press.

Freud, S. (1914). On narcissism: an introduction. *Stand[ard...]* Hogarth Press.

———. (1917). Mourning and Melancholia. *Standard*

Kernberg, O. (1975). *Borderline Conditions and Patholog[y...]* Aronson Inc.

Settlage, C.F. (1989). The interplay of therapeutic and treatment of children: an application of contem[porary...] *Psychoanalytic Inquiry* 9:375–396.

their individual experience. Their expert guidance and sage mentorship is a source of comforting enlightenment and added confidence. For those of us in the healing professions who share some aspect of the work in this field, their generosity and candor are causes for gratitude as they open to us the private world of their caring devotion to the well-being of the vulnerable children and adults we all try to reach.

Reviewing the presentations of the authors contributing to this volume has been very rewarding and a source of personal pleasure. Learning about the rich experiences, the expert counsel, and carefully considered views of such a distinguished group of psychoanalytic clinicians has indeed been illuminating. I have expressed my own views at various points in order to clarify or expand a few aspects of the material under discussion. In considering loss and the mourning after each experience that brings bereavement and grief, extensive use has been made of concepts of object relations and the normative lifelong dependence that characterizes human existence. From a perspective of internal organization serving autonomy, achievement of self and object constancy is the indispensable developmental milestone reached through the separation–individuation process. While the symbiotic mode of relatedness will permanently cast its long shadow on the self-object functions and needs that sustain us through our lifetime, we aspire to live as self-directed independent individuals in charge of our own destiny, free from the interferences of external forces and the control of their powerful influence.

To this bipolar view of dependence versus autonomy, here I will add a statement with respect to the establishment of boundaries in developmental progression, as in regression. When regression is utilized in the service of the ego, it provides for a creatively flexible transition from one stage to another, as seen in play, fantasy, dreams, and problem solving, as well as in the analytic situation, among many.

Separation-individuation as a process begins an extended course that establishes and consolidates the boundaries between the self and the object. The clarity and sharp definition of these boundaries are important requirements for internal equilibrium and homeostatic regulation that depend on stability and constancy of self and object representations.

Not only id and ego, conscious and unconscious, internal and external, fantasy and reality, but self and object, yes and no, physical and mental, past and present, as well as pain and pleasure are subject to the distinguishing and discriminative attributes of these boundaries. Primary process versus secondary process thinking as well as primary narcissism versus secondary narcissism are similarly distinguished and differentiated within the discriminating attributes of these boundaries.

Although well-defined and distinct, these boundaries are permeable and interpenetrable as the ego's synthetic function may access the contents of each area and the so-called transitional space between them. Boundaries may entail areas of overlap, merging, or fusion. They may be, at times, or in places, mutually exclusive, repelling or impenetrable.

If we think of phases of development or challenges in life as steps, challenges, or obstacles to be put behind, each threshold represents a new boundary to be traversed, be it interpersonal, intrapsychic, age specific, cultural, or self-imposed. Of these, some may be random events dictated by fate.

Many factors can determine the ability of an individual to pass these thresholds; they can also influence the essential features of the outcome. As developmental prototypes, all these elements, in isolation or combined, are at work, subsumed within the process of separation–individuation. An important aspect of this process and its culmination in the resolution of the rapprochement crisis entails establishing, testing, negotiating and traversing heretofore nonexistent boundaries. The acquisition of this capacity forms the foundation upon which resiliency and flexibility are based. It brings together the multitude of strands that combine to support the mechanisms and structures involved in homeostatic self-regulation. From here on, contending with every new challenge, living through each crisis, and surviving any act of fate rest

INDEX

upon this foundation and draw support and strength from the interweaving network of these elemental strands. When this foundation is faulty or these strands are vulnerable, every step is destabilizing and each obstacle is insurmountable.

Developmental steps constitute an ontogeny of a predetermined series of universal boundaries confronted by everyone. Loss, trauma, and unwelcome challenges of everyday life, on the other hand, may be randomly imposed boundaries that are unforeseen and unexpected. Ontogenetically predetermined during our normal development, randomly encountered as loss or trauma, culturally constituted as in rites of passage or social ranking, and even deliberately selected as personal goals and feats or acts of courage, we face and traverse these boundaries at a certain cost, and we hope with valuable gain. Successfully meeting the challenges of crossing these boundaries opens new horizons, creates new gains, and brings vitalizing strength. It brings us closer to self-actualization and earned fulfillment, deepens our wisdom, and broadens our understanding of the world of meanings as well as materials.

This success, however, depends on the adequacy of the fundamental elements that are the by-products of separation-individuation. A failure here leaves the individual at great risk. The impact of loss, normatively and developmentally, or traumatically and as an act of fate, as we have discussed, leave profound effects. These effects depend on a combination of factors. The age of the individual is the first important determining factor because of the developmental level and the maturity of available tools that are needed to deal with the impact. Second is the quality of past object relations as the source and generator of the internalized modes, structures, and identifications. The third, but perhaps not in this order, would be the individual's basic endowment that together with past object relation experiences constitute the internal resources and personal identity. And, the fourth essential element is the availability of external resources and favorable circumstances that are necessary, but not sufficient. If the foundation of self-regulation and narcissistic homeostasis is unstable, the individual is incapable of utilizing the resources of the environment in the service of repair and integration.

Loss and mourning, as critical and challenging boundaries, may be confronted at any age. The effects of their existential affliction can be searched by questioning what past experiences have combined with what quality of innate endowment to prepare the individual for this impact. What are the quality and quantity of those supportive elements that may be available for self-containment, reorganization, and recovery? How great is the individual's ability to bring about or to use such favorable conditions? Traversing these, as all other developmental or incidental boundaries, will be a matter of recapitulation of separation-individuation, which is the developmental dyadic template for this ability.

REFERENCES

Bowlby, J. (1961). Process of Mourning. *International Journal of Psycho-Analysis* 42:317–340.

Etezady, M.H. (1995). Narcissism: primary-secondary, fundamental, or obsolete? In *The Vulnerable Child, Vol. 2,* ed. T. Cohen, M.H. Etezady, and B. Pacella, pp. 3–9. New York: International Universities Press.

Freud, A. (1946). *The Ego and the Mechanisms of Defense.* New York: International Universities Press.

Freud, S. (1914). On narcissism: an introduction. *Standard Edition* 14:69–102. London: Hogarth Press.

———. (1917). Mourning and Melancholia. *Standard Edition* 14:237–258.

Kernberg, O. (1975). *Borderline Conditions and Pathological Narcissism.* New York: Jason Aronson Inc.

Settlage, C.F. (1989). The interplay of therapeutic and developmental process in the treatment of children: an application of contemporary object relations theory. *Psychoanalytic Inquiry* 9:375–396.

About The Author

Salman Akhtar, M.D., is Professor of Psychiatry at Jefferson Medical College, Lecturer on Psychiatry at Harvard Medical School, and Training and Supervising Analyst at the Psychoanalytic Center of Philadelphia. His more than 175 scientific publications also include eighteen edited or co-edited books. Dr. Akhtar is the recipient of the Journal of the American Psychoanalytic Association's Award (1995), the Margaret Mahler Literature Prize (1996), ASPP's Sigmund Freud Award (2000), and the Edith Sabshin Award of the American Psychoanalytic Association (2000).